B

DAP

EST

T0247219

Travel with Marco Polo
Insider Tips

INSIDER TIP
Your shortcut
to a great
experience

MARCO POLO
TOP HIGHLIGHTS

GELLÉRT BATHS ⭐
These thermal baths decked out in Art Nouveau style are by far the most beautiful in Budapest, both inside and out.

➤ p. 31

BUDA CASTLE ⭐
This monumental castle and palace complex houses multiple museums and sits high on Buda Castle Hill (photo).
📷 *Tip: Walk all the way to the back of the footbridge to snap a great panoramic shot with fewer tourists around.*

➤ p. 34

FISHERMAN'S BASTION ⭐
A great place to relax: fall in love with the city and this wonderful view.

➤ p. 36

MARGARET ISLAND ⭐
This island park is both a hub for relaxation and a trendy meeting place to party the night away.
📷 *Tip: Why not go in search of the 200-year-old plane tree? Its huge hanging branch looks like a swing and makes a beautiful motif for your photo.*

➤ p. 38

PARLIAMENT BUILDING ⭐
No ifs and buts about it. Despite the country's political turmoil, the neo-Gothic expanse of the parliament building remains a mesmerising sight.
📷 *Tip: Your best bet is to take a photo from the other side of the river. It's just one stop on the metro to Batthyány tér and then down to the banks of the Danube.*

➤ p. 39

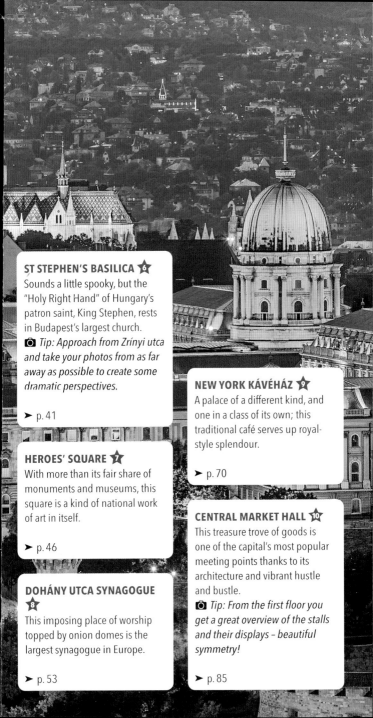

ST STEPHEN'S BASILICA ⭐6
Sounds a little spooky, but the "Holy Right Hand" of Hungary's patron saint, King Stephen, rests in Budapest's largest church.
📷 *Tip: Approach from Zrínyi utca and take your photos from as far away as possible to create some dramatic perspectives.*

➤ p. 41

HEROES' SQUARE ⭐7
With more than its fair share of monuments and museums, this square is a kind of national work of art in itself.

➤ p. 46

DOHÁNY UTCA SYNAGOGUE ⭐8
This imposing place of worship topped by onion domes is the largest synagogue in Europe.

➤ p. 53

NEW YORK KÁVÉHÁZ ⭐9
A palace of a different kind, and one in a class of its own; this traditional café serves up royal-style splendour.

➤ p. 70

CENTRAL MARKET HALL ⭐10
This treasure trove of goods is one of the capital's most popular meeting points thanks to its architecture and vibrant hustle and bustle.
📷 *Tip: From the first floor you get a great overview of the stalls and their displays – beautiful symmetry!*

➤ p. 85

CONTENTS

🕐   Plan your visit

€–€€€   Price ranges

(*)   Premium-rate telephone number

🌂   Rainy day activities

🐷   Budget activities

👪   Family activities

🚩   Classic experiences

(🗺 A2) Removable pull-out map
(🗺 a2) Additional inset maps on the pull-out map
(0) Off the map

CONTENTS

BEST OF
BUDAPEST

The view of parliament from the Fisherman's Bastion is strikingly beautiful

BEST ☂
WHEN IT RAINS

ACTIVITIES TO BRIGHTEN YOUR DAY

SHELTER FOR ART FANS
The *Hungarian National Gallery* has centuries' worth of paintings and sculptures to enjoy. The café and museum shop aren't to be scoffed at either.
➤ p. 34

BUDAPEST FROM BELOW
Budapest is a city of caves. In the Buda Hills visitors can go down into the *Pálvölgyi* and *Szemlőhegyi* caves and admire the capital from below.
➤ p. 58

SUNDAY BRUNCH
Rainy Sundays are best enjoyed at a slow pace. Head to *Déryné Bisztró* for its ample brunch, served in an elegant yet relaxing atmosphere, accompanied by live music.
➤ p. 70

BOOKWORM HEAVEN
The rain just makes reading better, doesn't it? *Massolit Books & Café* serves hot coffee and tea, and has a fantastic selection of books.
➤ p. 83

DELICIOUS FAST FOOD
The *Central Market Hall* sells every conceivable Hungarian culinary delicacy. Don't miss the *lángos* (photo) stall on the first floor: this is the place to experience just how tasty a deep-fried flatbread, with mashed potato often added to the dough, can be, especially when topped with grated cheese and sour cream.
➤ p. 85

HOPS & MALT
While you won't stay dry here, you will still escape the rain in an ingenious manner. The *Beer Spa* is everything you could wish for in bad weather: warmth, peace and quiet, and beer (including alcohol-free varieties).
➤ p. 106

BEST 🐷
ON A BUDGET

FOR SMALLER WALLETS

CULTURAL TREAT ON PUBLIC HOLIDAYS

To celebrate three public holidays, some of Budapest's best museums, including the *Museum of Fine Arts*, offer free admission to everyone on 15 March, 20 August and 23 October.
➤ p. 47

JAZZ WITH STYLE

Just a few minutes on foot from the Kálvin tér is an insider tip for all jazz – or even chamber music – fans: the *Opus Jazz Club*, with its home in the Budapest Music Center. The admission price is an absolute bargain and they are known to organise free concerts.
➤ p. 98

FITNESS FOR FREE

Work out for free at one of Budapest's downtown outdoor gyms, with equipment available to all. A popular venue,

especially among joggers, is the fitness park under Margaret Bridge.
➤ p. 107

SIGHTSEEING ON THE RAILS

Take *tram line 2* (photo) to experience everyday life in Budapest, along with great scenery. The best place to sit is on the Danube side for the full panorama from Margaret Bridge to the Palace of Arts. Try to avoid rush hour, when the tram gets too full.
➤ p. 130

THRIFTY EATS

Although thrilling, sightseeing can also be exhausting. If you get hungry between sights, head to the nearest restaurant and ask if they have a lunchtime or daily menu. Most restaurants serve them during the week and two or three courses are often available for just a handful of change.

BEST WITH CHILDREN

FUN FOR YOUNG & OLD

ON TOUR WITH A BRINGÓHINTÓ
You can hire these peculiar open vehicles on Margaret Island, where you can easily spend an entire day. *Bringóhintós* (photo) can be used by small children or families; electric or pedal-powered versions are available.
➤ p. 39

ISLAND SWIMMING
From wave pool to kids' pool: the *Palatinus Baths* on Margaret Island are bursting with fun for children and adults all year round. During high summer it tends to be very full, but in winter the outdoor pools are quieter and steam nicely.
➤ p. 39

PLAYGROUND OASIS
Looking for a quiet, secluded oasis in the middle of Pest city centre, where you can relax with the kids? *Károlyi kert* is a small park where dogs are not allowed. The playground was fully renovated in 2016, so children aged from two to 12 are sure to find something they enjoy here.
➤ p. 43

CHILDREN'S RAILWAY FUN
All aboard! The narrow-gauge railway, or *Gyermekvasút*, is operated by children (under supervision). The track through the woods is 11km long, and its stations are good starting points for hikes into the Buda Hills.
➤ p. 60

LEARNING THROUGH PLAY
That's the idea at the *Csodák Palotája (Palace of Wonders)* on the Buda side. A range of installations offer interactive science fun – and it's not just the kids whose curiosity will be piqued.
➤ p. 107

BEST ⚑

CLASSIC EXPERIENCES

ONLY IN BUDAPEST

FAIRYTALE CASTLE IN A FOREST
The fairytale *Vajdahunyad Castle* was built around 1900 in an imaginative mix of different architectural styles.
➤ p. 50

REMEMBRANCE & EXPERIENCE
The Moorish–Byzantine onion domes of *Dohány utca Synagogue* (photo) mark the heart of what was once the city's lively Jewish Quarter and is now a buzzing party district. The synagogue is a very handsome building, but it's also a memorial to those who suffered and perished during the times of the Budapest ghetto.
➤ p. 53

ICONIC BRIDGE
Spanning the Danube and weighing several thousand tons, the iron and stone *Liberty Bridge* is one of Budapest's best-known landmarks. During the day, hurrying locals and strolling tourists cross the bridge, while late in the evening, it's the perfect spot from which to watch the city fall asleep.
➤ p. 57

INCREDIBLE AMBIENCE
The *New York Kávéház* is brilliant! You should visit this café at least once, for it is the most breathtaking example of the Budapest grand café tradition. Other cafés may be cosier, but you'll not find anywhere with more overwhelmingly opulent decor to feast your eyes on over a cup of coffee.
➤ p. 70

COURTYARD SCENE
The courtyards of the old Jewish Quarter between Rákóczi út and Király utca are now the city's most popular nightlife locations. Buildings once threatened by decay have been turned into alternative-style "ruin pubs" – such as *Szimpla Kert*.
➤ p. 96

GET TO KNOW BUDAPEST

Take a break with the *Little Princess* on the Danube corso

DISCOVER BUDAPEST

Majolica roof tiles on the Museum of Applied Arts

However you choose to look at it – from above, from below or from the waters of the Danube – the city of Budapest is always spectacular. Admittedly, the city has its blemishes, from the crumbling plaster on its old buildings to the questionable politics played out in its Parliament, but visitors tend to fall in love with Budapest, warts and all. The view of the city at night from the Fishermen's Bastion is as hypnotising as a daytime tram ride through the streets and across the Liberty Bridge.

TWO FOR ONE
Some of the city's appeal lies in its division. Buda and Pest, the two juxtaposing halves of the city, are split by the River Danube and yet somehow united by their incongruous charm. Discover how the two sides differ in terms of their ambience,

1001
The Kingdom of Hungary founded by Stephen I

1541-1686
Ottoman rule: mosques and baths are constructed in the city

1867-1918
Austro-Hungarian Compromise, dual monarchy

1873
Buda, Pest and Óbuda unified; Budapest is born

1944
The German occupation of Hungary. Approx. 50,000 Jews deported from Budapest alone, approx. 70,000 deported to the Pest Ghetto

architecture and history. Yet what's certain is that the heights of the green Buda Hills and the retro urban flair of the Pest upper-class townhouses complement each other and belong together like two peas in a pod.

ONCE A CONSTRUCTION SITE...

Even a good 30 years after the fall of Communism in Hungary, Budapest is still a city in the midst of change and upheaval. It is striving for authenticity, modernity and a higher quality of life. The central squares, including Kossuth Lajos tér in front of the Parliament Building, have been renovated in recent years, while the Redoubt in Pest, along the banks of the Danube, has been restored to its former charm, as has the magnificent Franz Liszt Music Academy. The next large-scale building project on the city's agenda is "Liget Budapest": The municipal forest *(liget)* behind Heroes' Square is being redesigned into a kind of museum quarter. The House of Music and the Ethnographic Museum were opened here in 2022. The new National Gallery is still in the planning stages, while the Biodome, an extension of the zoo, is still under construction. But many Budapest locals are sceptical: building projects in Hungary are increasingly tainted by corruption, while hospitals and schools are left to fall into disrepair. Gergely Karácsony, the left-liberal-green mayor, is determined to put a halt to the remaining Liget construction plans in an attempt to preserve Budapest's "green lungs". However, it's questionable whether he will succeed in this, given the right-wing government's political supremacy.

1945
Battle for Budapest, Soviet troops take the city

23 October 1956
Popular uprising against the Communist government of the People's Republic of Hungary

1989
The Iron Curtain is lifted

2004
Hungary joins the EU

October 2019
Left-liberal-green Gergely Karácsony elected mayor

2022
Parliamentary elections; right-wing conservative Viktor Orbán re-elected as prime minister

STAY OR GO?

Known colloquially as the "Queen of the Danube", the capital is home to around 1.7 million people. This number speaks volumes about the city's significance when you consider that the entire population of Hungary is 9.8 million. Many Hungarians relocate from the provinces to the big city to study or in search of work and better living conditions, while more – especially singles under 40 – head further afield to Germany or Austria, where the euro beckons. However, some return due to homesickness. Take Ági for example. Born in Budapest, like many Hungarians of her age, this 28-year-old works for a multinational organisation. As a team leader she earns a net salary of 300,000 forints, a well-above-average Hungarian wage. With the help of a bank loan and her own savings, she has recently joined the property ladder as a first-time buyer and can finally stop paying the soaring rents in the capital.

NEVER A QUIET DAY

Budapest has the highest wages in the country. Yet it is almost impossible for most people to get rich from working. The cost of living is as high as in western European countries, but Hungarian wages only allow for a modest existence. Everyday life is tough for most people in Budapest. Nevertheless, they are their city's biggest fans. That is because Budapest is where the action is: international music stars only perform in the capital, and it is only here that major sporting events and festivals are held. The city is also the best departure point for travelling.

During the summer months Budapest is a veritable open-air mecca. The banks of the Danube, the municipal forest and the parks are all places the people of Budapest like to flock to in their free time. And it's not just young people – families like to get out and enjoy the outdoors too. Szilvi and Tomi are in their thirties and live with their two children in one of the prefab high-rise apartment blocks on the Buda side of the city. They have a tight budget, but there's no penny-pinching when it comes to quality time with their children. The zoo, the children's railway, rollerblading on Margaret Island and trips to the Buda Hills are all things this family enjoys. Join them, and pack your rollerblades, too!

YOUR TYPICAL CAPITAL

Márta is a representative of the older generation: she was born in Budapest and has remained loyal to the city her whole life. You'll often find her in her local coffee house. Chatting with her friends there, with a piece of *Dobos-torta,* is a must, she says, even though her monthly pension of 80,000 forints is not really enough to justify it. Among her other pleasures are visits to the *thermal baths.* Budapest's thermal baths are more than just spas – they are places to relax and socialise. A trip to Budapest would not be complete without experiencing a visit to a traditional coffee house and a thermal bath.

The glass walls of the Bálna cultural centre reflect modern life in the city

The people of Budapest may spend the week in the city, but during the summer months at least, the exodus begins on Fridays. The most popular destinations are the nearby Lake Velence, Lake Balaton and the Danube Bend. Some who enjoy a break from the city are those who managed to acquire a little holiday getaway during the country's Communist years, while others visit friends and relatives who live in the countryside.

A THOUSAND YEARS OF HISTORY

On the Feast of St Stephen of Hungary, the most important national holiday, celebrated on 20 August, hundreds of thousands of people from Budapest take to the streets, squares and bridges. History is omnipresent in the minds of everyone in Budapest. The city's story began in 896 with the "conquest" of the seven Magyar tribes under the leadership of Grand Prince Árpád. The first king of Hungary, Stephen I, whose coronation took place in AD 1000, is especially revered. The Crown of St Stephen is on display in the Hungarian Parliament building. After the Mongols overran the country in 1241–42, Béla IV of Hungary built the first fortress on Castle Hill. Matthias Corvinus, King of Hungary from 1458 to 1490, had it extended in the Renaissance style. This Golden Age was followed by almost 145 years of continuous occupation by the Turks (1541–1668). By the time the battle against the occupying power was won, Buda and Pest had been completely destroyed.

DEVASTATING CHAPTERS IN HISTORY

In 1941, Hungary took Germany's side in World War II against the Soviet Union. During the Nazi reign of terror, supported by the Hungarian Arrow Cross Party, Budapest's Jewish Quarter was turned into a ghetto and a graveyard for thousands. At the end of the war, large areas of the city lay in ruins. In 1947, the Communist Party came to power. Protests by students in Budapest triggered resistance against the regime in 1956, but the revolt of the "counter-revolutionaries" was brutally suppressed. Decades later, in the night leading up to 11 September 1989, Hungary opened its border with Austria, allowing around 100,000 East German citizens, many of whom had travelled to Hungary that summer, to escape to West Germany. On 23 October, on the 33rd anniversary of the Revolution of 1956, the Republic of Hungary was proclaimed from a window of the Hungarian Parliament Building. This marked the end of the Communist People's Republic.

URBAN DEVELOPMENT AT ANY PRICE

In recent decades, the spotlight in Budapest has focused mainly on the flourishing developments in the city: the wonderfully restored beacons of historic Budapest; the huge international investments in shopping centres and luxury real estate; and large projects such as the Millennium Quarter around Rákóczi Bridge. The darker sides of progress have tended to be ignored, however. The most recent economic crisis has increased public-sector financial problems, as well as social tensions. Even in liberal Budapest, the word "international" no longer has a positive ring to it. On the one hand, international corporations based in the capital are important investors and employers. But on the other hand, they also represent the banks, to whom many homeowners are in debt – with many residents in danger of losing their homes. As the country's political and economic centre, Budapest and its ills are viewed with a sharper focus than those of the nation as a whole.

PAST, PRESENT AND FUTURE

People are taking stock in the capital. The most important question is: how have the past 30 years benefited "ordinary" Hungarians? Budapest is focusing more than ever on the difficult living conditions of the majority and on the city's unique Hungarian identity. The people of the city want the Budapest of tomorrow to be different. What should it look like? The answer is not yet clear. Meanwhile, the beauty of the city remains untouched by all of this discussion. It seeps its way through the cracks in the crumbling house walls. It radiates from the charming courtyards in Pest and the refurbished metro stations, as well as from the ever-humorous Hungarians themselves. Are you smitten yet?

AT A GLANCE

1.75 MILLION
Population

Buda: 505,000, Pest: 1,244,000
London: approx. 9.65 million

81
museums
in Budapest
London: over 192

15.6km
Üllői út is the longest street in Budapest.
Green Lanes in London is 10.1km

18 PER CENT
of the Hungarian population lives in Budapest

HIGHEST POINT: JÁNOS-HEGY

527m
The chairlift takes 15 minutes to get to the top

THE FIRST

METRO LINE
in continental Europe was metro line 1 (Földalatti) – it is still in operation today

LOWEST POINT:

96m
The Danube at medium water level

PUBS AND RESTAURANTS IN THE CITY CENTRE

There are so many pubs in districts V and VI that all their residents could go out at once and still find a seat

Ó UTCA
Shortest street name –
the "Old Street" is in the VI district

SYNAGOGUE ON DOHÁNY UTCA
Europe's largest synagogue

TOMB OF GÜL BABA
THE NORTHERNMOST PILGRIMAGE SITE IN ISLAM

UNDERSTAND BUDAPEST

BUDA OR PEST?

Although people from Budapest are extremely proud of their magnificent city, it matters little to locals whether someone was born in Budapest or has moved here from the countryside. A far more telling fact is on which bank of the Danube they live. Despite the official unification of Buda, Óbuda and Pest in 1873, the "Buda versus Pest" debate as to which side of the city is better is still as heated today as it ever was.

Built on a series of green hills – including Gellért Hill and Castle Hill with Buda Castle – Buda is the calmer and prettier side. But Pest locals say that Buda inhabitants are snobbish, old and boring – at least, that's the cliché. In contrast, city centre Pest is the party and nightlife district – and too loud, dirty and grey for many Buda citizens, who only cross the river to work and go out in the evenings. Yet this unlikely pair can only be fully appreciated when seen as a united city. So take a stroll on a sunny day over the Margaret Bridge, enjoy the view of both banks of the Danube and listen to Róbert Rátonyis' love song "Budapest, Budapest, te csodás!" (Budapest, you are wonderful). Reconciliation guaranteed!

INVENTIVE FOLK

What do the ballpoint pen (Biro), Rubik's Cube (Rubik-kocka) and Vitamin C have in common? They were all invented or discovered by Hungarians! The Magyars are extremely proud of their inventive spirit, and only too happy to tell visitors about the momentous inventions that started life in their small country. Today, this spirit of innovation lives on in young Hungarian start-up companies, some of which have achieved international acclaim. For example, take Prezi, the digital presentation tool developed in 2007 by artist Ádám Somlai-Fischer and IT programmer Péter Halácsy; just two years after its founding, Prezi moved its headquarters to Silicon Valley and today it's used all over the world.

HIDDEN GEMS

Admittedly, the buildings are beautiful from the outside, but it's what's inside that really counts. Budapest is full of what are known as "ruin bars", which are well worth visiting. They are often set in and around the inner courtyards of dilapidated bourgeois houses in Pest or in former industrial buildings. These have been transformed into chic restaurants, pubs, clubs or hotels by entrepreneurial restaurateurs and hoteliers. With its splendid paved mosaic floor and plant-covered facades, the inner courtyard of the 1877-built *Almássy Palace (Almássy-palota, Ötpacsirta utca 2)* is an oasis in the middle of the city, housing the popular restaurant *Építészpince (epiteszpince.hu)*. And if

The Rubik's Cube is just one of the Hungarian inventions that has achieved international acclaim

INSIDER TIP
**Hidden
shopping**

you visit the confectioner Auguszt (see p. 66) make sure to take a peek into the courtyard, which is now home to *Paloma Artspace*, a co-working space with showrooms for dozens of artists and designers *(palomabudapest.hu)*.

UNDERGROUND WORLD

Can you imagine a room in which 350 double-decker buses would fit side by side? No, not an aircraft hangar but a gigantic, underwater labyrinth of caves right beneath the Buda side of Budapest. The city's historic thermal baths derive their heat from the hot thermal waters here. Budapest is home to the largest collection of thermal caves in the world. Divers with a cave-diving certificate can take part in

a guided diving session in warm waters of 21–27°C in the János Molnár cave. But you don't have to get wet to visit other caves: in district II, the stalactites and mineral formations in the Pálvölgyi and Szemlohegyi caves can be admired from dry land. There are even cave areas suitable for sufferers from claustrophobia: the Hospital in the Rock in the Castle district and the Gellért Rock Chapel.

THE POETRY OF COFFEE HOUSES

Cigarette smoke, heated discussions and the noise of turning newspapers: Budapest coffee houses were intellectual hotspots for writers, journalists and artists at the end of the 19th and beginning of the 20th century. Opened in 1894, the legendary New York Kávéház even offered poor writers free paper and ink. Today, there is little left of the authentic atmosphere, yet the magnificent interior, first-class service and amazing desserts, such as the *Dobos-torta*, more than compensate.

Sweet treats in Café Gerbeaud

RIVER ENCOUNTERS
The River Danube is both so near and yet so far in Budapest. Although it connects the two halves, Buda and Pest, stones and other barriers separate man from water almost everywhere in the capital. The best way to get close to the river is on a bike tour or by HÉV train along the northern bank to the Római-part (Roman banks) in the north of Buda. If you're travelling by bike, make a stop and let your feet dangle in the water at the open-air bar *Fellini*. At the annual dragon boat festival held in May on the Kopaszi gát peninsula, you can watch as others take to the water. The Danube is also the star on 20 August, St Stephen's day and a national holiday, when a dramatic fireworks display takes place over the water.

QUICK TONGUES
In Hungarian, the word for "quick-witted" is *talpraesett*. It translates literally as "fallen on your feet" – and not in luck but in humour. The people of the city always have a joke at hand and an opinion on everything.

UNDER ORBÁN'S IRON FIST
Right-wing extremism, dictatorship, Euroscepticism – these are just some of the less-flattering words used by the international press when writing about Hungary under Viktor Orbán. In 2019, the NGO Freedom House, which uses an index to measure the degree of democracy and freedom in countries around the globe, downgraded the country's status from "free" to "partly free" – a first since the fall of communism in 1990. Nevertheless, many Hungarians don't seem all that dissatisfied with domestic politics. Orbán's right-wing Christian nationalist party, Fidesz, was first elected in 2010 and has stayed in power ever since, with Orbán remaining in post as prime minister.

However, there are locals have also now had enough of "Orbánistan", and a government that has been responsible for corruption scandals and many absurd changes in legislation, while not bringing any real improvement to living standards. Poverty has been on the increase for years and the social gap is widening. Migration to countries abroad poses a serious problem for the Hungarian labour market. That said, party propaganda and dwindling media freedom cloud the picture, and statistics are sometimes falsified, so it's hard to tell what's really happening. As a result, many Hungarians quickly adopt a cynical tone when talking about domestic politics, and political disenchantment is growing. In autumn 2019, the wind of change seemed to be sweeping through the country when several Fidesz party mayors were voted out of office in local elections, to be replaced by opposition politicians. In the capital, the left-liberal-green Gergely Karácsony was able to hold his own with his promises to strive for a freer, fairer and more liveable Budapest. However, in 2021, he failed to become the opposition's prime ministerial candidate against Orbán's Fidesz party, and Fidesz went on to win the parliamentary elections in 2022.

ART NOUVEAU À LA BUDAPEST

The industrial boom that started in 1870 had a noticeable effect on Budapest's architecture and led to Hungary's own interpretation of Art Nouveau, which flourished at the turn of the 19th century. Hungarian Art Nouveau is characterised by ornate but not tacky decadence – it's a unique style, but one influenced by international architecture styles. It is no coincidence that the leading figure of Hungarian Art Nouveau, Ödön

TRUE OR FALSE?

PAPRIKA MAD

Powdered paprika on … well, just about everything? Visitors to Budapest love to return with tales of the city's inhabitants reaching into their pockets for the blood-red spice in a restaurant, and everyone knows Hungarians never travel abroad without some in their luggage, right? Urban myth or not, it is true that Hungarians hold the spice very close to their hearts (and plates). The paprika from the southern Hungarian towns of Kalocsa and Szeged is famous and a great buy from any good Budapest supermarket. Opt for hot *(csípős)*, sweet *(édes)* or smoky *(füstölt)*.

ORGANISED CHAOS

In many ways, Budapest is no different from any other European capital. It's modern, with its fair share of cosmopolitan inhabitants. Recycling has been practised for years, card payments are smooth in most shops and taxis. But then there's the other side to the city: the sheer chaos. Budapest has a wonderful talent for flexibility and turning a blind eye. But it can be frustrating when sensible rules and regulations are simply ignored … Tip: relax into it, let things happen and enjoy the adventure.

Lechner (1845–1914), is often referred to as the "Hungarian Gaudí" after the Catalan star architect, Antoni Gaudí.

The best way to admire the many examples of Art Nouveau architecture is to take a tour of the city. Several masterpieces can be found on the edge of Budapest's municipal forest, such as the *Egger Villa (Városligeti fasor 24)*. A secret gem is the large-scale building belonging to the Institute for Geography and Geophysics *(Magyar Földtani és Geofizikai Intézet, Stefánia út 14)*, designed by Lechner himself. The building is roofed with amazing sky-blue Zsolnay ceramic tiles and a gigantic globe supported by four figures. Both the inside and outside are adorned with spectacular folkloric decorative elements. It seems laughable that Franz Joseph I of Austria, on a state visit to Budapest, uttered his dissatisfaction with the building's exterior!

PREJUDICE & THE ROMANI PEOPLE

The Roma are an itinerant ethnic group originating from the Pannonian Basin in Central Europe. They are officially the largest ethnic minority in Hungary. Most of the Roma in Budapest have lived here for centuries and are no less Hungarian than their neighbours, yet they are still treated as outsiders. Every taxi driver can tell you prejudiced "truths" about the *cigányok* (gypsies) and will quickly

Swim like royalty in the palatial Széchenyi Baths

warn you against visiting districts inhabited by the Roma. In fact, the Roma, numbering around 600,000–800,000, make up a significant proportion of the Hungarian population. For many of them, music is an escape from the poverty and discrimination they face and, ironically, Roma musicians have traditionally been held in high esteem in the country. This tradition inspired the jazz guitarist Ferenc Snétberger to establish a centre for talented musicians *(snetbergercenter.org)*, which regularly organises concerts for young Roma people. The cultural centres *Auróra* and *Gólya* in district VIII also work hard to promote dialogue between the minority and majority populations.

ECCENTRIC LANGUAGE

Megszentségteleníthetetlenségeskedéseitekért – no, not a typing error, but with 44 letters it is officially the longest word in the Hungarian language. It means something like "for your continued behaviour as if you could not be desecrated". Unsurprisingly, it is almost never used but is still a good example of the complexity of the Hungarian language. Contrary to common belief, Hungarian does not belong to the Slavic but the Finno-Ugric family of languages. Like most other languages, it has started to borrow English words at an accelerated rate over the last few decades. Examples include *mobil*, *szponzor*, *szuper*, sport and muffin.

WARM-WATER SPRINGS

If you go looking, it is easy to find something to complain about when it comes to the rich thermal baths of Budapest: the Király Baths are a tad musty and may look a little rough around the edges, but then they do date back to the Ottoman period. And despite the rotten egg odour of the sulphur water basin at the Rudas Baths, you can still have a great deal of fun in these natural healing waters. The outdoor pool at the Széchenyi Baths is fantastic in winter when a thick misty fog develops above the water caused by the cold outside temperatures. Quite the spectacle! Or simply go to the Gellért Baths to watch the dignified old men and women in their bathing caps swim their lengths.

INSIDER TIP
Natural smoke machine

SIGHT SEEING

"I am from San Francisco, and San Francisco is the most beautiful city, but Budapest isn't far behind." That was Tom Hanks' verdict when he came to the Hungarian capital for a film shoot a few years back. In fact, many people would argue that Budapest is more beautiful than any US rival. You will certainly struggle to decide what to visit first. Do you start back in medieval times at the Castle in Buda? With the neo-Renaissance St Stephen's Basilica in Pest? Or in modern times with contemporary architecture at the *Bálna*? You could just follow your appetite and start with a large, deep-fried *lángos* topped

A charmed trio: the Danube, the Chain Bridge and the Parliament Building

with soured cream and cheese. Don't panic: whatever you decide, you'll have enough time to pack in all the sights, even if you're only staying in Budapest for a long weekend.

The city was made to be explored on foot. And don't forget to look up: although they sometimes appear decaying and crumbling at first glance, the city's buildings are often fascinating, with ornamental Art Nouveau details and amusing, pathos-heavy statues. Perhaps you'll spot a kitsch retro store sign or even the odd cat staring down at you from a balcony above.

NEIGHBOURHOODS AT A GLANCE

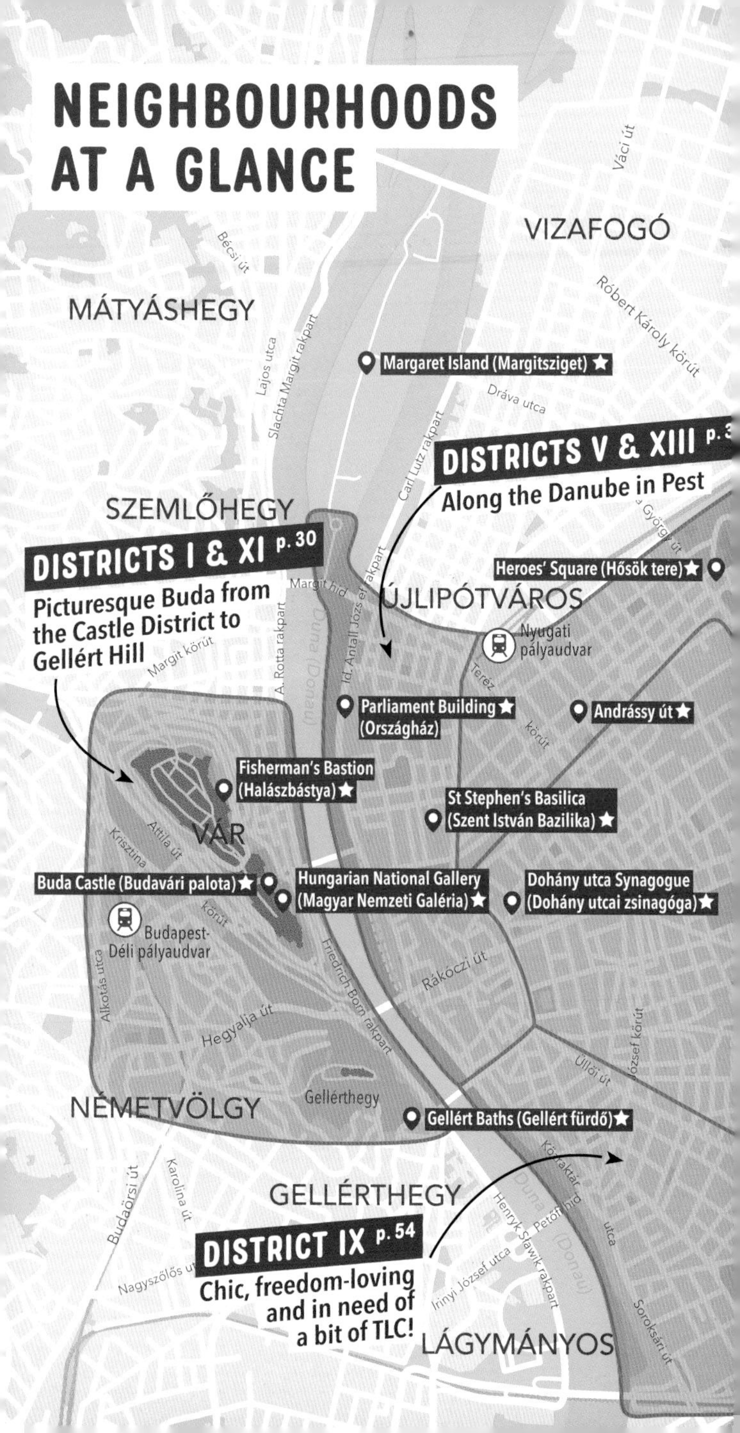

VIZAFOGÓ
Váci út
Bécsi út
MÁTYÁSHEGY
Róbert Károly körút
Lajos utca
Slachta Margit rakpart
Margaret Island (Margitsziget)
Dráva utca
Carl Lutz rakpart
DISTRICTS V & XIII p. 3
Along the Danube in Pest
SZEMLŐHEGY
DISTRICTS I & XI p. 30
Picturesque Buda from the Castle District to Gellért Hill
Margit híd
Heroes' Square (Hősök tere)
ÚJLIPÓTVÁROS
Nyugati pályaudvar
Margit körút
A. Rotta rakpart
Duna (Donau)
Id. Antall József rakpart
Teréz körút
Parliament Building (Országház)
Andrássy út
Fisherman's Bastion (Halászbástya)
St Stephen's Basilica (Szent István Bazilika)
VÁR
Attila út
Krisztina körút
Buda Castle (Budavári palota)
Hungarian National Gallery (Magyar Nemzeti Galéria)
Dohány utca Synagogue (Dohány utcai zsinagóga)
Budapest-Déli pályaudvar
Alkotás utca
Friedrich Born rakpart
Rákóczi út
Hegyalja út
József körút
Üllői út
Gellérthegy
NÉMETVÖLGY
Gellért Baths (Gellért fürdő)
Közraktár utca
Budaörsi út
Karolina út
GELLÉRTHEGY
Petőfi híd
Henryk Sławik rakpart
DISTRICT IX p. 54
Chic, freedom-loving and in need of a bit of TLC!
Nagyszőlős út
Irinyi József utca
Soroksári út
LÁGYMÁNYOS

MÁV-TELEP

ANGYALFÖLD

DISTRICTS VI & XIV p. 44
Historic buildings meet pleasure gardens

HERMINAMEZŐ

Városliget

ISTVÁNMEZŐ

DISTRICTS VII & VIII p. 50
Clubs, bars and religious heritage in the Jewish Quarter

KEREPESDŰLŐ

JÓZSEFVÁROS

Népliget

GYÁRDŰLŐ

Nagy Lajos király útja
Csömöri út
Kacsó
Thököly út
Hungária körút
Kerepesi út
Fiumei út
Kőbányai út
Könyves Kálmán körút
Gyömrői út
Üllői út

1 km
0.62 mi

MARCO POLO HIGHLIGHTS

★ **GELLÉRT BATHS**
Relax in one of Hungary's most beautiful thermal baths ➤ p. 31

★ **BUDA CASTLE**
The massive complex towers above the city and the river ➤ p. 34

★ **HUNGARIAN NATIONAL GALLERY**
An overview of Hungary's art ➤ p. 34

★ **FISHERMAN'S BASTION**
You'll have the best views of the city from up here ➤ p. 36

★ **MARGARET ISLAND**
Budapest's green lung ➤ p. 38

★ **PARLIAMENT BUILDING**
The city's most imposing landmark is located beside the Danube ➤ p. 39

★ **ST STEPHEN'S BASILICA**
The enormous dome of this impressive church reaches almost 100m into the sky ➤ p. 41

★ **ANDRÁSSY ÚT**
The magnificent avenue leading to Heroes' Square ➤ p. 44

★ **HEROES' SQUARE**
Take a crash-course in Hungarian history on Budapest's largest square ➤ p. 46

★ **DOHÁNY UTCA SYNAGOGUE**
A spectacular building and the largest synagogue in Europe ➤ p. 53

All in all, Budapest is an eclectic mix of **ruggedness and unshaven charm.** One moment you are firmly in the city's past enjoying a sweet slice of *Dobos-torta* in a coffee house – while the next you are abruptly confronted by the city's present with the sad sight of many homeless people living on the streets. In the wake of a rather cruel law passed by the Fidesz government, homeless people should no longer exist and are banned from living on the streets. Fortunately, the Budapest police leave them alone for the most part. You can help the city's homeless population by purchasing the Hungarian equivalent of *The Big Issue*, called *FN (Fedél nélkül,* "Without a cover") for a donation (the recommended minimum is 300 forints) – the sellers get to keep all their takings.

WHERE TO START?

Vörösmarty tér *(▥ D9)*: Vörösmarty Square in Pest is an ideal starting point for exploring the city. The elegant white building on the northwest side houses the legendary Café Gerbeaud. A highlight to the north of the square is St Stephen's Basilica, while the shopping street Váci utca can be found to the south. The panorama from the nearby Danube Corso is stunning: the views across the river extend from Gellért Hill along Castle Hill all the way to the Chain Bridge. Vörösmarty tér is served by metro line 1 *(Földalatti).*

DISTRICTS I & XI

Districts I (Budavár/Buda Castle) and XI (Újbuda/New Buda) are located on the west bank of the Danube. They also include parts of the Buda Hills in the hinterland, one of the city's preferred residential and recreational areas.

Be prepared to snap a lot of photos here! Visitors and locals particularly enjoy exploring the sites close to the Danube, first and foremost the Castle District. Of District I's 25,000 inhabitants, 2,500 still live in the alleys of the Castle District. The larger Castle Hill area is a fascinating mix. You will find parts of the Baroque town, traces of the medieval town and a lot of showy architecture from the 19th century. The underground world of Castle Hill is also quite striking. A vast system of passageways extends deep into the hill for several kilometres.

The Castle District's southern neighbour is Gellért Hill in District XI (population 145,000), with the Citadel and the imposing *Liberty Statue* visible from afar. As is demonstrated by its highly symbolic monuments, not to mention the outstanding architecture of the Gellért Hotel (once the city's most sought-after grand hotel), the section of District XI close to the city centre is one of the grandest parts of Budapest. With its exclusive villas, Gellért Hill is one of the city's most expensive residential areas.

1 GELLÉRT BATHS (GELLÉRT FÜRDŐ) ★

A bathhouse that looks as if it came straight out of a Wes Anderson film. The decorative Art Nouveau style welcomes guests in the entrance area and the inside walls are covered in magnificent mosaics. The thermal baths are a popular retreat for old Hungarian men and women and (especially) tourists. The 👪 outdoor wave pool was a sensation when it was built almost 100 years ago. *Daily 9am-7pm | admission Mon-Fri 7100 Ft., Sat/Sun 7600 Ft. | online tickets (to avoid queueing): jegyek. gellertfurdo.hu | Kelenhegyi út 4 | gellertbath.hu | metro 4 Szent Gellért tér | tram 19, 41, 47, 48, 49, 56 | District XI | ⅏ d11*

2 GELLÉRT ROCK CHAPEL (GELLÉRT-HEGYI SZIKLATEMPLOM)

The small chapel, beautifully situated in the side of Gellért Hill, is a cosy retreat, and not just for believers. On the forecourt is a lovely statue of King Stephen holding a small model of the church in his hands. From here, you have a stunning view of the Liberty Bridge and the Danube. Once inside, you will find an oasis of tranquillity at a constant 21°C. But it wasn't always this peaceful: the rock church and neighbouring Paulite monastery were shut down under Communism and the monks were deported by the Hungarian state police on Easter Monday 1951. Today, three monks still call the rock home and organise the church services here. They request participation or silence during the services (8.30am, 5pm and 8pm, Sun also 11am). *Daily 9.30am-7.30pm | admission 750 Ft. | Szent Gellért*

The Liberty statue on Gellért Hill is a prominent landmark

rakpart | up staircase near Gellért Baths | metro 4 Szent Gellért tér | tram 19, 41, 47, 48, 49, 56 | District XI | ⏱ 20 mins | ⅏ d11

3 LIBERTY STATUE (SZABADSÁG SZOBOR)

Although branded by some locals as the "Bottle Opener", Zsigmond Strobl's 14m-high statue of a lady raising a palm frond and proclaiming freedom is a special landmark. Some of her fame is attributed to the local legend surrounding her; namely that Miklós Horthy, Hungarian governor from 1920 to 1944, originally wanted her to carry a propeller blade in memory of his son who died in a plane crash during the war. Another reason for the lady's popularity is the amazing view over Budapest, the Danube and its bridges from the foot of this bronze statue erected in 1947. Your best bet is to head out in the evening when the majority of tourists are replaced by the young people of Budapest, who like to meet here. *Citadella sétány | bus 27 Búsuló Juhász (Citadella) or on foot from Szent Gellért tér | District XI | ⌂ c11*

INSIDER TIP
Young Budapest!

⓸ RUDAS BATHS (RUDAS FÜRDŐ)

Old meets new at Rudas, at the foot of Gellért Hill: the thermal springs at this location were first mentioned as far back as 1292, but it is the architectural footprint of the Turks from the 16th century that you still see today, in the dome, for example.

The beautiful baths have been comprehensively restored and modernised, with a wellness and sauna area added a few years back. The highlight, however, is the small panorama pool on the roof which offers a fantastic view of the Danube on one side and Gellért Hill on the other. The adjoining *Rudas Bistro* restaurant also has a great view. Why not treat yourself to a goulash soup or poppy seed strudel after your swim? Particularly unusual are the nocturnal bathing times at the

INSIDER TIP
Swim and snack

A beautiful place to unwind: Rudas Baths

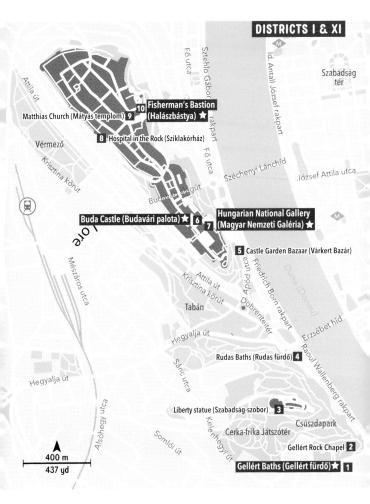

DISTRICTS I & XI

Matthias Church (Mátyás templom) **9**

10 Fisherman's Bastion (Halászbástya) ★

8 Hospital in the Rock (Sziklakórház)

Buda Castle (Budavári palota) ★ **6**

7 Hungarian National Gallery (Magyar Nemzeti Galéria) ★

5 Castle Garden Bazaar (Várkert Bazár)

Rudas Baths (Rudas fürdő) **4**

Liberty statue (Szabadság-szobor) **3**

Gellért Rock Chapel **2**

Gellért Baths (Gellért fürdő) ★ **1**

▲
400 m
437 yd

---

weekend. *Tue women only, Mon, Wed-Fri until 10.45am men only | night swimming (without sauna) Fri, Sat 10pm-3am (everyone) | admission Mon-Fri from 6500 Ft., Sat/Sun from 8500 Ft., night swimming 8600 Ft. | Döbrentei tér 9 | de.rudasfurdo. hu | tram 19, 41, 56 Rudas Gyógyfürdő | bus 7 | District I | ▭ c11*

5 CASTLE GARDEN BAZAAR (VÁRKERT BAZÁR)

Are you fed up following the crowds, dashing from one attraction to the next, and would prefer to simply hang out for a while? Then head to the Castle Garden Bazaar on the banks of the Danube beneath the castle. If the word bazaar conjures up images of the bustling markets in Istanbul, you are not too far from the truth – as far as the past is concerned. Following the bazaar's completion in 1883, the site was not only a busy trading place, but the building complex with gardens also housed artists' studios. The bazaar was designed by Miklós Ybl, one of the most talented Hungarian architects of his time, and completely renovated between 2011 and 2014. The garden and open-air area is open from 6am to midnight and is particularly enchanting in the evenings when it's illuminated. Exhibitions and concerts are also held in the gardens. Stairs (and lifts for those in a rush) take you up Castle Hill. *Daily | Ybl Miklós tér 2-6 | varkertbazar.hu | tram 19, 41 Várkert Bazár | bus 16, 105 Clark Ádám tér | District I |* ⏱ *30 mins | ▥ c10*

INSIDER TIP
Stairs or lift?

6 BUDA CASTLE (BUDAVÁRI PALOTA) ★

There's a lot to discover up here. First and foremost, the spectacular view over Budapest and the Danube as it weaves its way through the city and under the bridges that connect the city's two halves. The city's history is also depicted by the beautifully decorative statues dotted around the gardens. What else can we say … Oh yes, Buda Castle (also known as the Royal Palace) is Hungary's largest building and it's easy to lose your way around here – as many Budapest locals do. But don't worry – you can't get irrevocably lost: the entire complex is just 1.5km long. The castle, the

city's monumental landmark and once its royal palace, was destroyed three times between the 13th and 20th centuries, but always rebuilt in the style of the particular era – originally with Gothic elements, later with Renaissance and Baroque ones. An interesting mixture!

Buda Castle now houses the Hungarian National Gallery, the *History Museum (Tue–Sun 10am–6pm | admission 2400 Ft.)* and the National Széchenyi Library. While you are up here, keep a lookout for the monstrous bird known as the Turul! This mythological creature is said to have dug its claws into a sword on the edge of the Szent György tér in front of the palace and is now a national symbol for Hungary. If you need a breather, go to the viewing platform just metres away, above the tunnel that runs under the Castle Hill. Sit back and relax on a bench as you watch the world go by on Clark Ádám tér and the Chain Bridge. *Castle Palace grounds: daily | free admission | Szent György tér | bus 16, 16A, 116 Dísz tér | bus 105 Clark Ádám tér, then funicular | District I |* ⏱ *30 mins (without the museums) | ▥ b-c 9-10*

INSIDER TIP
Hilltop views

7 HUNGARIAN NATIONAL GALLERY (MAGYAR NEMZETI GALÉRIA) ★ 🛆

Be warned: you can literally spend hours in the National Gallery, home to a vast collection of Hungarian fine art and international art from 1800 onwards. If you don't have so much time (or energy) to spare, concentrate

Promenade with a view: treat yourself to a stroll in front of the Castle Palace

on the section exhibiting works by Mihály Munkácsy (1844–1900). Hungarians are proud of the Hungarian-born realist painter of international acclaim. Among the permanent exhibits are Gothic wooden sculptures, panel paintings and late-Gothic winged altars (more exciting than they sound!).

If you have made the trip here, it's worth visiting the museum shop, where you can buy an excellent colouring book about the National Gallery and its treasures, entitled *A colourful journey in the Hungarian National Gallery* by Viola Varga and Anita Nemes. It also sells "POPpins",

fun badges by designer Ramóna Udvardi, which are great to take back home as souvenirs. Your ticket will give you access to the dome on the third floor of Wing C, which has fantastic views. In good weather you can even step out onto the dome's terrace. *Tue–Sun 10am–6pm | admission 3400 Ft | Szent György tér 2 | Buda Castle wings A, B, C and D | en.mng.hu | funicular | bus 16, 16A, 116 Dísz tér | District I | ⏱ 3 hrs | ⊞ b9*

🔟 HOSPITAL IN THE ROCK (SZIKLAKÓRHÁZ)

Kill two birds with one stone with an intriguing glimpse into both

Budapest's underground world and recent Hungarian history. You will learn all about what was for a long time a state secret known only by the code name LOSK 0101/1: a military hospital with an operating theatre and the government's nuclear bunker. The caves were also used during World War II by the Nazis, and during the Hungarian Revolution of 1956. Incidentally, Robert de Niro was also impressed by the hospital in the rock – and especially by the potential of activating the air raid siren – on a visit to Budapest. *Daily 10am–7pm | visit only with a guided tour (hourly) | admission 5000 Ft. | Lovas út 4c | sziklakorhaz.eu/en | bus 16, 16A, 116 Dísz tér, 105 Clark Ádám tér | District I | ⏱ 1 hr | ▱ b9*

❾ MATTHIAS CHURCH (MÁTYÁS TEMPLOM)

Your first impressn of St Matthias may well be that it looks like something out of a fairy tale. Even the square in front – the Szentháromság tér (Trinity Square) – is so enchanting that you may find it hard to pack your camera away. And then there is the church itself – a gem of Neo-Gothic architecture. It is named after King Matthias Corvinus, who still bears the epithet "the Just" today. During the Turkish occupation it was used as a mosque, but in 1867, it became royal again: the Austrian imperial couple Franz Joseph I and Elisabeth (Sisi) were crowned, making them king and queen of Hungary.

The entrance fee is hefty but well worth it; the inside of this 700-year-

old church is just as impressive as the outside. If you're looking for a new motif for your next panoramic shot of Budapest, then climb up the 80m bell tower. You will be rewarded with a magnificent bird's eye view. For a special experience, a children's choir usually sings sacred music here on Fridays at noon (for example, works by Franz Schubert, but also Hungarian composers). *Mon-Fri 9am–5pm, Sat 9am–noon, Sun 1pm–5pm | admission for tourists 2000 Ft., bell tower 2200 Ft. extra | Szentháromság tér | matyas-templom.hu | bus 16, 16A, 116 Dísz tér | District I | ⏱ 30 mins | ▱ b8*

❿ FISHERMAN'S BASTION (HALÁSZBÁSTYA) ★

You could spend hours up here, mesmerised by the city's stunning panorama and the grandiose neo-Romanesque architecture of the Fisherman's Bastion. The viewing platforms, towers, walkways and archways, all in white-grey stone, belong to a fairy-tale castle and were designed by the architect Frigyes Schulek and built between 1895 and 1902.

Don't come here expecting to see fish though – the name is a reminder of the fact that there were once defensive walls here that were secured and defended by the guild of fishermen in the Middle Ages. *Main viewing platform 9am–7pm, otherwise always accessible | free admission all day, except upper platform area 1000 Ft. | Szentháromság tér | bus 16, 16A, 116 Dísz tér | District I | ⏱ 20 mins | ▱ b8*

700 years old and pretty as a picture: the view of the Matthias Church is magical

DISTRICTS V & XIII

So much magnificence in just one square mile! Almost all of District V (Belváros-Lipótváros) is made up of listed buildings – no fewer than 294 of them. It is home to some of Hungary's most outstanding attractions.

Wealth, both sacred and profane, is on show in the magnificent buildings near the Parliament, including the monumental St Stephen's Basilica. One example of luxurious hotel architecture is Gresham Palace (now the Four Seasons Hotel), housed in a wonderful Art Nouveau building.

District V, the heart of Pest, has just under 26,000 inhabitants. As well as more than its fair share of impressive architecture, it is a great option for having fun, eating and drinking. Still, the population here is definitely aging and the district is increasingly swamped by tourists. Architect Dalma Faddi neatly summarises district V as a "shop window district".

To the north is District XIII (including Újlipotváros, population: 121,000), of which Margaret Island, the city's green lung, is part. It has streets of 19th-century townhouses, and the area around Pozsonyi út has a trendy east London vibe. On the whole, though, the district is characterised by working-class tenements and national minorities.

11 MARGARET ISLAND (MARGITSZIGET) ★

It doesn't cost a penny to visit this popular Budapest attraction and it's worth visiting by day or by night, whatever the season. The island is neither Buda nor Pest, floating directly in the middle of both in the Danube. It can be reached from the north over the

Árpád Bridge (not particularly pretty) and from the south over the Margaret Bridge (very pretty). Stretching for 2.5km, and 0.5km wide, the island is perhaps the only place in Budapest that locals can agree on – it attracts the whole spectrum of the population, from after-work joggers, teenage skate-boarders, tourists, expats and trendy cool types with beards, to grandmas in wheelchairs.

Autumn is the time to stroll among the falling leaves, collecting chestnuts, while in summer visitors get around on funny four-wheel covered bikes known as 🚲 *bringóhintós (March–Sept Mon–Fri 8am–5pm, Sat/Sun 9am–5pm | pedal car from 4880 Ft., electric 5580 Ft./children 4880 Ft., small children 3480 Ft. per hour | rental point: to the south end of the island by the fountain north of the Japanese garden | bringohinto.hu)*. In winter when it snows, a wonderful silence descends here, unlike anywhere else in the city. For old and young alike, there are (unfortunately rather mediocre) pubs, clubs, restaurants, delicious *lángos*, ice-cream and candy floss, a Japanese garden and even a mini-zoo *(15th March–4th Nov daily 10am–6pm | free admission)*.

Whatever season you choose, the 🚲 *Palatinus Baths (Palatinus fürdő) (daily 8am–7pm | admission Mon–Fri 3500 Ft., Sat/Sun 4,000 Ft., children 3-14 2,900 Ft. or 3,300 Ft., parts cheaper in winter | de.palatinusstrand. hu)* are great fun with thermal, wave and kids' pools, as well as saunas. Don't underestimate the four water slides. They're great fun, but depending on your weight they can be quite a ride!

Other popular attractions include the open-air theatre and musical fountain at the southern tip of the island. The main landmark on Margaret Island is the water tower, a listed building with viewing platform (worth climbing up even if most locals don't

do it). *Tram 4, 6 | bus 26, 226 Margitsziget/Margit híd | District XIII | 🗺 C-D 3-6*

🔟 SHOES ON THE DANUBE BANK (CIPŐK A DUNA-PARTON)

Empty pair after empty pair of metal shoes stand on the banks of the Danube, right in front of the water. This symbolic memorial by Gyula Pauer and Can Togay commemorates the mass shootings of mainly Jewish Budapest residents in 1944 and 1945 by Hungarian fascists. Most victims were taken from the ghetto to the Danube and murdered in cold blood by Arrow Cross soldiers along the banks of the river. The afternoon is not the best time to reflect on this moving memorial, as this is when it's most popular with tourists. For more peace and quiet, try the morning. *Antall József rakpart | metro 2 Kossuth Lajos tér | tram 2 | District V | 🗺 c8*

🔟 PARLIAMENT BUILDING (ORSZÁGHÁZ) ★

"Is it for sale? How many bedrooms has it got?" was apparently what Freddie Mercury jokingly asked in 1986 when he saw the gigantic Parliament Building during a boat trip on the Danube. (The answer: no, and 700 rooms.) No surprise really – whether from water or on land, the building, designed by architect Imre Steindl (1839-1902), with its neo-Gothic elements, is a bombastic piece of architecture designed to impress. Its inside is equally grand. Among the many political ideologies represented in the Hungarian Parliament, there

Crowned with its mighty dome, St Stephen's Basilica is the largest church in Budapest

was perhaps none so lasting as state socialism, which was responsible for symbolic red star present on the 96m-high dome between 1950 and 1990. Now turn around and walk towards the Ministry of Agriculture, just a few feet away and also on Kossuth tér. Can you spot the little bronze balls on the wall of the building? They are supposed to symbolise bullet holes, to memorialise the shooting of unarmed demonstrators here on the square on 25 October 1956. You can visit an exhibition on the history of the Parliament for free at the end of the tour, while the remaining exhibitions (Lapidarium and In memoriam 1956) are open to all free of charge. *April–Oct daily 8am–4pm, English guided tours daily | admission EU citizens 4200 Ft.,*

INSIDER TIP
Memorial to the 1956 uprising

non-EU citizens 8400 Ft. | online tickets (good for avoiding queues): jegymester. hu/parlament | ticket office in the visitors' centre (underground on the north side of the Parliament building) | Kossuth Lajos tér | parlament.hu/ web/visitors | metro 2 Kossuth Lajos tér | tram 2 | District V | ⏱ guided tour 50 mins, with exhibition in the visitors' centre 1½ hrs | ▥ *c8*

🄳 SZABADSÁG TÉR (LIBERTY SQUARE)

Expansive Liberty Square, to the south of the Hungarian Parliament, is home to memorials including an enormous obelisk topped with a gold star (a 1946 memorial to the fallen of the Soviet Army), along with a bronze statue of Ronald Reagan (2011) and the antifascist Memorial for the Victims of the German Occupation. This latter monument depicts Hungary as the Archangel Gabriel being attacked by a German imperial eagle. Placed here in 2014 and funded by the Fidesz government, it is a controversial piece. Many Hungarians, including those representing Jewish community organisations, argue that it absolves Hungarian fascists of complicity in the Holocaust. Protesters were so disgusted that they erected an alternative memorial directly in front of it, which is updated regularly. Exciting! *metro 2: Kossuth Lajos tér | tram 2 | District V | ᙏ D8*

INSIDER TIP
Another perspective

15 ST STEPHEN'S BASILICA (SZENT ISTVÁN BAZILIKA) ★

Construction of this enormous neoclassical church lasted from 1867 to 1906. Its dome is 96m high. It collapsed in 1868 and destroyed the building, which was half-finished at the time. The church's most significant art works are the statues by Alajos Stróbl, the altarpiece by Gyula Benczúr and the dome painting. The view from the dome's viewing platform is magnificent. You can take a lift up, after which you will also have to climb some stairs. A significant religious relic, the mummified hand of King Stephen, is exhibited in the basilica, and to the right of the entrance is the way down to the treasure chambers. Discover the church's cultural programme (with the likes of organ and choir concerts) on site or at *bazilika. biz/en*. *Mon 9am–4.30pm, Tue–Sat 9am–5.45pm, Sun 1–5.45pm | admission 1200 Ft. for the church only,*

2200 Ft. for viewing platform and treasure chambers, 3200 Ft. combi ticket | Szent István tér | metro 1: Bajcsy-Zsilinszky út | metro 3: Arany János utca| District V | ᙏ 1 hr | ᙏ D9

16 SZÉCHENYI ISTVÁN TÉR

Roosevelt Square – it's worth remembering this alternative name, too, as it's what most locals still call the square. after the former US president, even though it was officially renamed Széchenyi tér back in 2001. On the Pest side of the Chain Bridge the square is primarily worth seeing thanks to two imposing buildings: *Gresham Palace*, which now houses the Four Seasons Hotel (and of course regular visitors from Hollywood and the world of music), and the striking neo-Renaissance building that houses the Hungarian Academy of Sciences *(Magyar Tudományos Akadémia)* or MTA. The latter is a hive of activity, with some of the country's best brains working away, including scientists collaborating with Audi on the car of the future. The MTA also brings us neatly full circle back to Count István Széchenyi, who generously offered a year's yield from his land to fund the establishment of the academy back in 1825. *tram 2 | bus 105, 178 Széchenyi István tér | District V | ᙏ c9*

17 SZÉCHENYI CHAIN BRIDGE (SZÉCHENYI LÁNCHÍD)

Without doubt this stunning bridge is a favourite among most Budapest locals as well as tourists. First opened to traffic back in 1849, it had been undergoing renovations for some time, and finally reopened in August 2023 with improvements including wider pavements and LED lighting. Make sure to take a look at the lion statues at either end of the bridge. Legend has it sculptor János Marschalkó committed suicide when he realised he had forgotten to carve tongues on his lions. Fortunately, the story is just that: an urban legend! *District V* | c9

INSIDER TIP
An urban myth

18 DANUBE CORSO (DUNAKORZÓ)

It's time to don your best Belle Époque outfit, including an extravagant hat, and take up your walking stick for a stroll along Budapest's posh promenade. The Duna Korzó, or Danube Corso, stretches between Széchenyi Chain Bridge and Elizabeth Bridge. On the Pest side of the city, the riverside promenade is reminiscent of the extravagance of the Belle Époque era – it's lined with extortionately priced restaurants and hotels, as well as imposing buildings such as the Pest Redoubt. Don't forget to take a photo of yourself posing with the bronze statuette of the *Little Princess* sitting on the railings ... *District V* | c–d 9–10

19 PEST REDOUBT (PESTI VIGADÓ)

Wagner, Debussy, Liszt – many of the great composers have performed in this gigantic venue, opened in 1865 as a ballroom and concert hall. The Redoubt is worth seeing if only for its ornately decorated façade and neo-Romanesque style. It's also a great place to catch a concert or exhibition. We recommend the in-house restaurant *VígVarjú* if you get peckish while you're there: the 🐷 lunch specials are great value! *Daily 10am–7pm | admission 1500 Ft. | Vigadó tér 2 | vigado.hu | metro 1: Vörösmarty tér | tram 2: Vigadó tér | District V | ⏱ 1 hr | c–d9*

20 VÖRÖSMARTY TÉR

In the middle of the square is a memorial to the poet Mihály Vörösmarty (1800–55). The splendid monument is made of high-quality Carrara marble. At the front end, opposite Váci utca, is the renowned Café Gerbeaud. *metro 1: Vörösmarty tér | District V | d9*

21 VÁCI UTCA

This shopping street between Vörösmarty tér, Ferenciek tere and Fővám tér is a magnet for visitors. You will find the usual international chain stores typical of such thoroughfares here. The pedestrianised southern section, running all the way to Fővám tér, has its own flair, with an array of interesting stores, including fashion boutiques and antique shops. *metro 1: Vörösmarty tér | metro 3: Ferenciek tere, metro 4: Fővám tér | District V | d9–11*

22 INNER CITY PARISH CHURCH (BELVÁROSI PLÉBÁNIATEMPLOM)

Just a bit to your right, please! Perhaps the most famous anecdote surrounding this Roman Catholic church is that there were plans at the start of the 20th century to move it by a few metres to accommodate the Erzsébet (Elizabeth) Bridge. As you can see, the two are nestled very close together today! A visit to this place of worship is like stepping back in time, offering an insight into its 2000-year old history: you can see the crypt dating from Roman times through the plexiglass floor of the nave (you can also go down and visit it), view one of the frescoes dating from the 14th century and even discover the Muslim prayer niche, the *mihrab* – a legacy of the Ottoman Empire when the church was used as a mosque. *Mon–Sat 9am–5pm, only outside service times | admission 2600 Ft. (includes upper and lower church, and observation tower) | Március 15. tér | belvarosi plebania.hu | metro 3: Ferenciek tere | tram: 2 Március 15. tér | District V | ⏱ 30 mins | ⌗ d10*

**INSIDER TIP
See a Roman crypt**

🖾 KÁROLYI KERT 👪

Quiet, secluded oasis in the middle of the hustle and bustle of Pest city centre. This small park is surrounded by wrought-iron fencing and dogs are not allowed, so it is safe for little ones to run around. Kids have a choice of two playgrounds, while mums and dads can enjoy a refreshing lemonade or a cold brew at one of the surrounding cafes. Child and parent-friendly! *Ferenczy István utca | metro 2: Astoria | tram 47, 49 | District V | ⌗ e10*

🖾 UNIVERSITY SQUARE (EGYETEM TÉR)

Since it has been closed to traffic, this square in the city's south has regained

Café Gerbeaud on Vörösmarty tér

a lot of its former charm. Home to the Central University and the Károlyi Palace, the square offers several cafés and the small park *Károlyi Kert* is just a few feet away. The *University Church (Egyetemi templom)* is also located around the corner, a Baroque masterpiece from the middle of the 18th century. The delicate frescoes and the pulpit are particularly worthy of note. *metro 3, 4: Kálvin tér | tram 47, 48, 49 | District V | ⌗ d–e10*

DISTRICTS VI & XIV

District VI (Terézváros) boasts a special mix of culture and hip events. The main highlight here is the boulevard Andrássy út.

High art mingles with popular culture on and around Andrássy út. For example the Opera House, the Academy of Music and the Operetta Theatre are all located here. The restaurant and café scene in the district (pop. 39,000) is just as lively, particularly on Liszt Ferenc tér, known as "Budapest's Broadway".

With Budapest's most imposing square, Heroes' Square, at the northeastern end of Andrássy út and the adjoining municipal forest, District XIV (Zugló, population: 124,000) has two of the capital's major attractions to call its own.

25 ANDRÁSSY ÚT ★

Do you realise you're trampling on a UNESCO World Heritage Site? You don't need to tread carefully though – just appreciate the amazing architecture flanking this 2.5km-long boulevard. Alternatively, take the underground, known locally as *Földalatti*, which also has its charms. The tram is small, the carriages are short and the doors close so quickly that you can barely get in before they shut on you. Opened in 1896, it is the oldest underground in continental Europe. Back above ground on Andrássy út, also known as the "Champs Élysées of Budapest", you pass various sections as you stroll down from your starting point at the Bajcsy-Zsilinszky út crossroads to the end at the vast Heroes' Square. Lined at the start with diverse luxury stores, you walk past the delightful Opera House and restaurants then begin to pop up on both your left and right. From the Oktogon onwards, the avenue becomes quieter and the architecture more elegant until it reaches the Millennium Monument where the sheer size of Heroes' Square will bowl you over. *District VI |* 🗺 *D–F 7–9*

26 OPERA HOUSE (OPERAHÁZ) 🛡

The magnificent neo-Renaissance Opera House, constructed between 1875 and 1884, is a work by architect Miklos Ybl, who also drew up plans for the entire length of Andrássy út. It is not just the Opera's façade that is stunningly beautiful, but the opulent interior as well. The Opera House finally reopened to the public in 2022 after a good five years of renovations. Still, the modernisation and reconstruction saw details regilded and the acoustics in the main hall improved – and it was worth it! Interestingly, letters from the 1880s and 1890s were also discovered during the renovation work. *Andrássy út 22 | opera.hu | metro 1: Opera | District VI |* 🗺 *D–E8*

27 LISZT FERENC TÉR

This 200m-long square centres around a green strip of park and is flanked by cafes and restaurants: more a street

The gleaming interior of the Opera House

than a conventional square, Liszt Ferenc tér is a secluded corner in this otherwise bustling area of the city centre. Named after the piano virtuoso and composer Franz Liszt (1811–86), the square commemorates him with two statues – one in the middle to commemorate the 100th anniversary of his death and a bronze statuette on the splendid Liszt Ferenc Music Academy on the corner of Király utca.

INSIDER TIP
Coffee and people-watching

Order a coffee or ice cream in one of the cafés here and watch the comings and goings in the bustling square. *metro 1: Oktogon | tram 4, 6 | District VI | E8*

🕮 OKTOGON

Situated at the intersection of Andrássy útca and Térez körút, this busy octagonal square is among Budapest's most attractive squares, lined by 19th-century apartment blocks. Also a popular choice as a place to start a night out! *metro 1: Oktogon | tram: 4, 6 | District VI | E8*

🕮 HOUSE OF TERROR (TERROR HÁZA)

The House of Terror is a memorial to the victims of 20th-century persecution, illustrating the grim decades of Jewish and Roma persecution under the Nazis and further repression and misery under the Communists. It is housed in the very building where, from 1937 onwards, the Nazi secret police established their headquarters. Countless people were physically and psychologically broken, tortured to death, or executed in the building's basement. After the end of World War II, the Hungarian secret service and security organisations took over the premises, torturing, executing or deporting people to Soviet camps. *Tue–Sun 10am–6pm | admission 3,000 Ft. | Andrássy út 60 | terrorhaza.hu/en | metro 1: Oktogon | tram: 4, 6 | District VI | ⏲ 2½–3 hrs | 🕮 E8*

30 HEROES' SQUARE (HŐSÖK TERE) ★

Heroes' Square, on the northeastern end of Andrássy út, is the city's largest square and combines national pride with aesthetics to produce an impressive whole. The 36m-high column in the middle of the square, the Millennium Memorial, commemorates the 1,000th anniversary of the creation of the Hungarian nation in 896. Parliament decided to commission a monument in 1896, but 33 years passed before it was finally completed in 1929. Archangel Gabriel stands up on the column. He allegedly ordered King Stephen in a dream to convert Hungary to Christianity; today he watches skateboarders zooming over the square. The statues in the two colonnade arches are of heroes from Hungary's history. The square's other central elements are two classical-style monumental buildings: the Hall of Art and the Museum of Fine Arts. *metro 1: Hősök tere | bus 20E, 30, 30A, 105, 178, 230 | Trolleybus 75, 79M | District XIV | 🕮 G6*

The House of Terror remembers the victims of a succession of cruel 20th-century regimes

DISTRICTS VI & XIV

Budapest Zoo (Budapesti Állatkert) **33**

Széchenyi Baths **34** (Széchenyi fürdő)

Museum of Fine Arts **31** (Szépművészeti Múzeum)

Heroes' Square (Hősök tere) ★ **30**

Vajdahunyad Castle **35** (Vajdahunyadvár)

Municipal Forest **32** (Városliget)

House of Terror **29** (Terror háza)

25 Andrássy út ★

28 Oktogon

27 Liszt Ferenc tér

26 Opera House (Operaház)

400 m
437 yd

31 MUSEUM OF FINE ARTS (SZÉPMŰVÉSZETI MÚZEUM)

If you prefer classic to contemporary, then this museum is for you. The museum building is over 100 years old but its collection dates back a lot further, with Egyptian, Greek and Roman artefacts and a large selection of Italian paintings. In the past, it has housed internationally acclaimed exhibitions featuring artists from Picasso and Salvador Dalí to Frida Kahlo, Michelangelo and Toulouse-Lautrec. The museum was recently extensively renovated and modernised. Among other treats, you can now learn about almost 300 works of art on the world's largest LCD video wall! *Tue-Sun 10am–6pm | admission 3,400 Ft., EU citizens under 27 1,600 Ft., over-62s 1,700 Ft. | Dózsa György út 41 | mfab.hu | metro 1: Hősök tere | bus 20E, 30, 30A, 105, 178, 230 Trolleybus 75, 79M | District XIV | ⏱ 2–3 hrs | 🗺 F–G6*

🟥 MUNICIPAL FOREST (VÁROSLIGET)

Endless space and many treasures to discover: the extensive 100-hectare park is dotted with interesting attractions such as Vajdahunyad Castle, the Széchenyi Baths and Budapest Zoo.

The municipal forest experienced its heyday as an attraction between 1867 and 1914, when it functioned as a pleasure garden. Everyone, from the lowliest maids and servants to aristocratic ladies and gentlemen, flocked to the park for amusement or a simple stroll. Today, the people of Budapest love the park for its boating in the summer and ice-skating in the winter *(ice rink usually Nov–late Feb Mon–Fri 9am–1pm and 5–9pm, Sat 10am–2pm and 4–9pm, Sun 10am–2pm and 4–8pm | admission Mon–Fri mornings 1,500 Ft., Fri pm–Sun 2,000 Ft. | skate hire*

> **INSIDER TIP**
> **Boating and skating**

Summer fun on the lake in the municipal forest

2,500 Ft. plus 2,000 Ft. deposit, double blade skates/skating aids for children 500 Ft. each | Olof Palme sétány 5 | mujegpalya.hu/en).

The equivalent of several hundred million pounds has been invested, and a lot of work has already been done, on the controversial Liget Budapest construction project. While its supporters proclaim it as the largest cultural project in Europe, civil activists and opposition politicians see it rather as an environmentally damaging waste of money, not least as the development will see significant cuts to the green space of the public park.

Whatever you make of it all, it's hard to deny that some of what has been built here does look impressive, such as the *House of Music (Zene háza)*, which nestles between the trees like a gigantic white gold mushroom. Among other functions, it is home to an outdoor stage, a concert hall and a fun, interactive museum. Next door is its 🎭 musical playground, which has been a great success. If you've brought the kids, you absolutely have to come here. *Metro: 1 Hősök tere and Széchenyi fürdő | Bus 20E, 30, 30A, 105, 178, 230 Hősök tere, trolleybus 75, 79M Hősök tere | 72M Széchenyi fürdő | District XIV | ⚏ G–H 6–7*

🟥 BUDAPEST ZOO (BUDAPESTI ÁLLATKERT) 🎭

Located in the urban forest and founded in 1866, the zoo not only houses many exotic animals but is also an architectural gem with amazing Art Nouveau buildings. Special attractions include the richly adorned elephant house and the palm house dating back to the start of the 20th century. The colourful tiles were produced by the famous Southern Hungarian Zsolnay tile and porcelain company. The Pallas's cat, born in 2022 and a species of cat from Central Asia, is also a big crowd-puller.

Not too long ago, the zoo took over the grounds of the former amusement park, the *Holnemvolt Park (holnem voltvar.hu)*; some of its listed heritage attractions are open to visitors in summer. Once construction is complete there will be more to see in the *Biodome* (part of the Liget Budapest construction project). *Core opening hours daily 9am–4pm | admission 3,300 Ft., children (2–18) 2,200 Ft., under-2s 200 Ft., family ticket (2 adults and 1 child) 8,000 Ft. | Állatkerti körút 6–12 | zoobudapest.com | metro 1: Széchenyi fürdő | District XIV | ⏱ 3 hrs | ⚏ F–G6*

🟥 SZÉCHENYI BATHS (SZÉCHENYI FÜRDŐ)

These sunshine-yellow baths resemble a magnificent palace complex. There are 12 indoor and three outdoor pools, as well as saunas, steam cabins, a buffet and massage options. There are also fun *ColorBath (colorbath.hu)* events on Friday evenings – something between a light show and a relaxed party. Special events aside, it is simply great fun to sit in one of the open-air pools and enjoy the warm thermal water. You'll need a bit of luck to get a spot by one of the chessboards in the pools, however. Bring your own towel and flip-flops to avoid buying on site. *Mon–Sat 7am–8pm | day ticket incl. cabin use Mon–Fri 7,100 Ft., Sat/ Sun 7,600 Ft. | Állatkerti körút 11 | szechenyibad.hu | metro 1: Széchenyi fürdő | trolleybus 72M | District XIV | ⌖ G6*

35 VAJDAHUNYAD CASTLE (VAJDAHUNYADVÁR) ⚑

Budapest's answer to Disneyland! This medieval-looking castle in the municipal forest was actually built in the 19th century – originally as a wooden model for the Budapest Millenium Exhibition in 1896, before being memorialised in stone in 1908. The architect took his inspiration from Hungary's traditional architectural styles, which is why different parts of the building echo Romanesque, Gothic, Renaissance and Baroque styles. The main inspiration, however was Hunedoara castle (Vajdahunyadi vár) in Transylvania. The castle houses a large *agricultural museum (Mezőgazdasági Múzeum | Tue–Sat 10am–5pm | admission 2500 Ft. | mezogazdasagimuzeum.hu)*, also in the Baroque style. Its exhibits can be a little on the dull side, but the magnificently furnished rooms are well worth seeing.

INSIDER TIP
Views from two towers

Alternatively, opt to just visit the two towers – *Kaputorony* (Gate Tower) and *Apostolok tornya* (Apostle Tower) – and soak up the views *(daily | admission Kaputorony 300 Ft., Apostolok tornya 600 Ft.)*. While you need a guide to visit the latter, its view is admittedly more impressive. *Vajdahunyad sétány | metro 1:*

Széchenyi fürdő | trolleybus 72M | District XIV | ⌖ approx. 2 hrs | ⌖ G6

DISTRICTS VII & VIII

The lively dining hub of Gozsdu Court is not the only hip spot along Király utca. Most of this trendy street is officially still part of district VI, but it's also the starting point for discovering district VII (Erzsébetváros, population: 52,000), home to the old Jewish Quarter.

As well as providing reminders of the past, District VII is all about optimism for the future. This part of the city used to be dominated by Jewish life, particularly between Király utca and Dohány utca. Today, it is well on its way to combining tradition and modernity. With its mix of cool designer shops and kosher restaurants, hip bars and shops selling Jewish religious artefacts, magnificently restored houses and still-visible decay: the neighbourhood developing here has its own very special flair. The district is also associated with the development of Hungarian literature, inextricably linked with the New York coffee house. The famous café, immaculately restored after closure during the Communist era, glows in its former glory, but literary figures are no longer seen here. Today, writers and other creatives meet in the popular "ruin pubs" of the former Jewish Quarter.

41 Gozsdu Court (Gozsdu udvar)

42 Orthodox Synagogue (Ortodox zsinagóga)

40 Rumbach Synagogue (Rumbach Sebestyén utcai zsinagóga)

39 Dohány utca Synagogue (Dohány utcai zsinagóga) ★

38 Hungarian National Museum (Magyar Nemzeti Múzeum)

400 m
437 yd

Erzsébet körút

Rákóczi út

Kiss József utca

II. János Pál pápa tér Fiumei út Cemetery **37**

Fiumei út

Népszínház utca

Teleki László tér

Mátyás tér

Baross utca

József körút

Károly körút

Múzeum körút

Vámház körút

Üllői út

Közraktár utca

Ferenc körút

Mester utca

Duna (Donau)

Nehru Part

Közösségi Park

Üllői út

Hungarian Natural History Museum (Magyar természettudományi Múzeum) **36**

District VIII (Józsefváros/Joseph Town, 77,000 inhabitants) was home to the literary elite of the country in the 1930s, but had become an extensive working-class quarter. However, things are now changing and urban grittiness is gradually giving way to gentrification. That holds particularly true for the student-oriented Palace Quarter around the National Museum. Anyone wanting to see the modernisation process for themselves should explore a few of the streets around Gutenberg tér (near Blaha Lujza tér).

Among the rows of houses there are some wonderfully restored buildings. Between them, however, are some that still look just as they did after the Second World War.

36 HUNGARIAN NATURAL HISTORY MUSEUM (MAGYAR TERMÉSZETTUDOMÁNYI MÚZEUM) 😎

The neoclassical museum complex is a fascinating place. The glass floor leading up to the exhibition lets visitors look down on coral reefs, while

Gozsdu Court in the Jewish Quarter is ideal for evening exploration

a three-ton skeleton of a fin whale hangs from the domed ceiling of the entrance foyer. The "Treasures of the Carpathian Basin" collection brings a world of myths and legends to life. *Thur–Sun 10am–8pm | admission 2,600 Ft., 6–26 years 1,300 Ft | Ludovika tér 2–6 | nhmus.hu/2n | metro 3: Semmelweis Klinikák | District VIII | ⏱ 1½–2 hrs | ☐ H12*

③⑦ FIUMEI ÚT CEMETERY (FIUMEI ÚTI SÍRKERT)

You could almost describe this cemetery (also known as Kerepesi temető) as a giant sculpture park. The decorative graves here are something else! Several important 19th-century politicians are buried in this famous cemetery, set in parkland with many mature trees. Lajos Kossuth, an activist during the Hungarian Revolution of 1848, has an imposing mausoleum. Poets and thinkers also lie here, including the novelist Jókai Mór (1825–1904, Lot 18) and the poet Ady Endre (1877–1919, Lot 19/1). Lot 19 also contains the grave of Hungarian-American film producer Andy Vajna, who died in 2019. At the eastern edge of the cemetery, with its tree-lined avenues, is an old *Jewish cemetery (Salgótarjáni utcai zsidó temető)* with impressive mausoleums. *Fiumei úti sírkert daily 7am–5pm, Salgótarjáni utcai zsidó temető daily 8am–2pm | Fiumei út 16–18 | metro 2, 4: Keleti pályaudvar | tram 2M 24, 28, 28A Dologház utca | fiumeiutisirkert.nori.gov.hu |*

INSIDER TIP
Discover the Jewish cemetery

zsidotemeto.nori.gov.hu | *District VIII* | ⊞ *H–J 9–10*

38 HUNGARIAN NATIONAL MUSEUM (MAGYAR NEMZETI MÚZEUM)

Take a moment before entering the museum to admire the building from the outside, with its splendid gardens and broad flight of steps – popular spot for students from the nearby ELTE university and ideal for a quick coffee before you start on the vast collection inside. Opened in 1847, the museum houses an immense collection of artefacts and relics. The best way to explore it is to start in the basement and work your way up through the various eras in Hungarian history. Most visitors particularly enjoy the exhibition covering the period from the end of the Second World War to the fall of Communism. The museum is immensely proud to own the coronation mantle of King Stephen, Hungary's first king. *Tue–Thur, Sat/Sun 10am–6pm, Fri 10am–10pm* | *admission 2,900 Ft.* | *Múzeum körút 14–16* | *mnm.hu/2* | *metro 3, 4: Kálvin tér* | *tram 47, 48, 49* | *District VIII* | ⏲ *2 hrs* | ⊞ *e10*

39 DOHÁNY UTCA SYNAGOGUE (DOHÁNY UTCAI ZSINA GÓGA) ★ ⚑

It is the largest synagogue in Europe and one of the city's most magnificent buildings. Located in Dohány utca, it was at the heart of Jewish life in Budapest after its completion in 1859. Built in the Byzantine-Moorish style with onion domes, it belongs to Neolog Judaism, a liberal Hungarian Jewish movement. In its courtyard, where the *Holocaust Memorial* by the sculptor Imre Varga is located – a silver, shimmering tree of life – thousands of victims of fascism lie buried. One of the wings houses the *Jewish Museum (Zsidó Múzeum* | *zsidomuseum.hu)*, which has a rich collection of Judaica dating from Roman times to the 20th century. It was built on the site of the house where Theodor Herzl (1860–1904), the founder of Zionism, was born. Keep an eye out for an electricity pylon on the synagogue forecourt, where artist Mihály Kolodko has immortalised Theodor Herzl with his bicycle in a guerrilla action in a miniature statue. Shoulders must be covered to enter the synagogue and men must wear a kippah. *May–Oct Sun–Thu 10am–6pm, Fri until 4pm or earlier, closed public holidays* | *admission 7,000 Ft., guided tour included* | *tickets from jewish tourhungary.com/de* | *Dohány utca 2* | *dohanystreetsynagogue.hu* | *metro 2: Astoria* | *tram 47, 48, 49* | *District VII* | ⏲ *1½ hrs* | ⊞ *e9*

INSIDER TIP
Guerrilla art

40 RUMBACH SYNAGOGUE (RUMBACH SEBESTYÉN UTCAI ZSINAGÓGA)

Budapest? Or Granada? A fair question, as the beautiful, towering façade of the Rumbach Synagogue shows strong Arabic influences. This place of worship, an early work by the Viennese Art Nouveau architect Otto Wagner (1841–1918), is owned by the Budapest Jewish Religious

Community (BZSH). It has been extensively restored over several years and has been open to the public in all its new glory since 2021. *Tickets at jewish tourhungary.com/de, combined tickets available with Dohány utca Synagogue | Rumbach Sebestyén utca 11-13 | metro 1, 2, 3: Deák Ferenc tér | tram 47, 48, 49 | District VII | ◫ e9*

🔢 GOZSDU COURT (GOZSDU UDVAR)

Manó Gozsdu was the Romanian who gave his name to this imposing 1902 building. Gozsdu Court on the edge of the old Jewish Quarter is an architectural masterpiece which runs from Király utca 13 to Dob utca. The long complex consists of seven building with six interlinking courtyards. Visitors can stroll from one courtyard to the next.

Many pleasant restaurants and cafés have settled in the complex and turned Gozsdu Court into a lively hotspot, particularly in the evening. We recommend *Sáo* (the *bún*-noodle soup is amazing) or stylish tapas bar *Vicky Barcelona*, before heading to neighbouring *Jardín* for cocktails. *Király utca 13/Dob utca 16 | gozsdu udvar.hu | metro 1, 2, 3: Deák Ferenc tér | District VII | ◫ e9*

🔢 ORTHODOX SYNAGOGUE (ORTODOX ZSINAGÓGA)

The Orthodox Synagogue looks humungous from the outside. One of three large synagogues in the Jewish District, it was erected in Art Nouveau style between 1911 and 1913 for the Orthodox community. Because of

its address, it is also known as the Kazinczy Street Synagogue, and you can find many Jewish buildings and stores in the area around it. It has been lovingly restored and can house up to 1,000 worshippers. *March-Oct Sun-Thu 10am-6pm, Fri until 4pm, April-Oct Sun-Thur 10am-4pm, Fri until 1pm | admission 1,000 Ft. | Kazinczy utca 29-31 | metro 2: Astoria | tram 47, 47B, 48, 49 | District VII | ⏱ 30 mins | ◫ e9*

DISTRICT IX

District IX (Ferencváros) has undergone a revival. Its central attraction is Ráday utca, with its cafés, restaurants, boutiques, and book and music shops.

The city's young and young at heart like coming here because Ráday utca and the surrounding area also have good, affordable living space. At the southern end of this district (pop. 60,000) is a project which, when completed, will confirm the reputation of this part of town as the capital's new cultural centre: the Millennium Quarter, with the National Theatre and the Palace of Arts. Although district IX is popular, there is still a lot of work to be done, particularly in the southern residential neighbourhoods. Hundreds of houses need demolishing, while 2,500 are in need of renovation.

43 PALACE OF ARTS (MŰVÉSZETEK PALOTÁJA)

With its large glass façade, the Palace of Arts is an impressive piece of contemporary architecture. If you can't manage to catch a concert in the Béla Bartók National Concert Hall or an exhibition at the Ludwig Museum for Contemporary Art, take a walk to see the snail sculpture in front of the palace or enjoy a stroll along the Danube. *Komor Marcell utca 1 | mupa. hu/en | tram 2, 24 Müpa-Nemzeti Színház | ⌁ F14*

44 LUDWIG MUSEUM (LUDWIG MÚZEUM)

Ever considered getting an electric shock from a work of art? Curious to see some post-Soviet installation art? Or how about a photo exhibition about the Beat Generation? Boredom will not be an issue in the Ludwig Museum, with its ever-changing exhibitions that are invariably well received. Budapest owes this important collection of contemporary international art to the collectors Irene and Peter Ludwig from Aachen in Germany. *Tue–Sun 10am–8pm | admission 3,400 Ft., exhibitions 1,600 Ft. | Komor Marcell utca 1 | ludwigmuseum.*

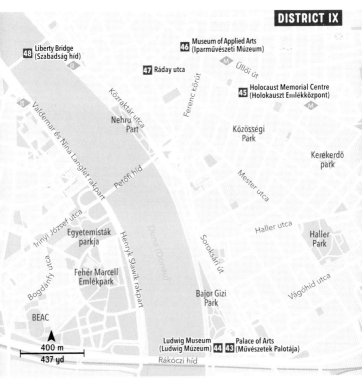

DISTRICT IX

48 Liberty Bridge (Szabadság híd)

46 Museum of Applied Arts (Iparművészeti Múzeum)

47 Ráday utca

Üllői út

45 Holocaust Memorial Centre (Holokauszt Emlékközpont)

Közraktár utca

Nehru Part

Valdemar és Nina Langlet rakpart

Petőfi híd

Ferenc körút

Közösségi Park

Kerekerdő park

Mester utca

Irinyi József utca

Egyetemisták parkja

Henryk Slawik rakpart

Duna (Donau)

Haller utca

Haller Park

Soroksári út

Bogdánfy utca

Fehér Marcell Emlékpark

Vágóhíd utca

Bajor Gizi Park

BEAC

400 m
437 yd

Ludwig Museum (Ludwig Múzeum) 44 43 Palace of Arts (Művészetek Palotája)

Rákóczi híd

hu/en | tram 2, 24 Müpa-Nemzeti Színház | ⏱ 2 hrs | ☐ F14

45 HOLOCAUST MEMORIAL CENTRE (HOLOKAUSZTEMLÉKÖZPONT)

This complex consists of the historic Páva Synagogue (you can visit it at the end of the exhibition) and a new wing dominated by glass. The interior deals with something much darker: the Holocaust in Hungary. In spring 1944, under the rule of Regent Miklós Horthy, 440,000 people were deported to Auschwitz. The Germans and the Arrow Cross Party (the Hungarian Nazis), who came to power in autumn 1944, were responsible for the deaths of tens of thousands more people. In total, the number of murdered Hungarian Jews and Roma is estimated at over 600,000. Darkness, the light in the cabinets, nightmarish sounds such as the footsteps of concentration camp guards: the exhibition is a journey from darkness to the synagogue's light domed room and out into the light of day. *Tue–Sun 10am–6pm | admission 2,400 Ft. | Páva utca 39 | hdke.hu/en | metro 3: Corvinnegyed | tram 4, 6 | ⏱ 2 hrs | ☐ F12*

46 MUSEUM OF APPLIED ARTS (IPARMŰVÉSZETI MÚZEUM)

The exhibits inside may not be everyone's cup of tea, but the building is worth a sneak peek for its magnificent Art Nouveau architecture, with its green ceramic tiled roof, elegant pure white atrium in the entrance area and oriental-style details. The museum is currently closed for renovation and expansion (reopening planned for 2025–26), but it is still definitely worth a look at the exterior. *Üllöi út 33–37 | imm.hu | metro 3: Corvinnegyed | tram 4, 6 | ☐ F11*

The sky above, the Danube below – young Budapest loves Liberty Bridge

47 RÁDAY UTCA
The traffic-calmed pedestrian zone Ráday utca, which has become a popular nightlife destination because of its many cafés and restaurants, begins at Kálvin tér. *Metro 3, 4: Kálvin tér | tram 47, 48, 49 | e11*

48 LIBERTY BRIDGE (SZABADSÁG HÍD) ⚑
"Let's meet up on the bridge," is a popular phrase among students and young people when summer evenings grow longer. They're talking about the green cantilevered *Szabihíd*, as the locals like to refer to Liberty Bridge. Crowds gather in the middle of the bridge, where the metal construction is low enough to sit on with a bit of manoeuvring, to enjoy striking views over the Danube with a drink in hand. The bridge is closed to car traffic and public transport on certain weekends in summer to allow picnickers, acrobats, longboard skaters and hammock enthusiasts to come and hang out undisturbed. There is even yoga, live music and film screenings *(FB: szabihid)*. What a great sense of liberty! *d11*

OTHER SIGHTS

49 MEMENTO PARK
How small you feel in comparison to the statues of the great figures of Communism (Marx, Engels, Lenin) and other socialist realist-style monuments that have been relocated from around the city to their final resting place here. This outdoor sculpture park includes an old Trabant car (photo opportunity!). There is also an indoor exhibition that provides more historical background information. Despite its distance from the city centre, it is a great place to visit if you're interested in relics and oddities from the Communist era. For a bit of fun, you can also embark on a Trabant tour to *Memento Park (mementopark.hu/en/information/trabant-transfer). May–Oct daily 10am–6pm, Nov–April 10am–4pm | admission 1,800 Ft. | corner Balatoni út/Szabadkai utca | mementopark.hu/en | bus 101B, 101E and 150 from station and metro station Kelenföld vasútállomás (Mon–Fri approx. every 10 mins, Sat/Sun every 30 mins) | tickets for programme with guided tour are available on the bus | District XXII | ⏱ 1½ hrs | 0*

50 KIRÁLY BATHS (KIRÁLY FÜRDŐ)
Király means king, and although they're small in size, the Király Baths are the prettiest thermal baths in Budapest for many locals because of their authentic Ottoman influences (they were built in 1565 under the orders of Pasa Arslan). Check the website before visiting as the baths have been undergoing major renovations and expansion since 2020 and will remain closed until construction is complete. *Fő utca 84 | en.kiralyfurdo.hu | bus 109 Kacsa utca | tram 19, 41 Bem József tér | District II | B7*

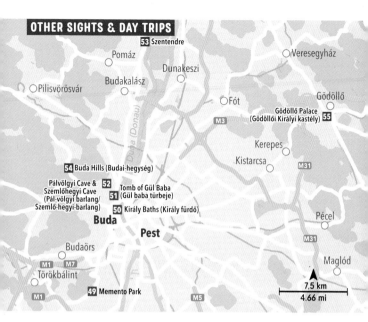

OTHER SIGHTS & DAY TRIPS

- 53 Szentendre
- Pomáz
- Dunakeszi
- Veresegyház
- Pilisvörösvár
- Budakalász
- Fót
- Gödöllő
- Gödöllő Palace (Gödöllői Királyi kastély) 55
- Kerepes
- Kistarcsa
- 54 Buda Hills (Budai-hegység)
- Pálvölgyi Cave & Szemlőhegyi Cave (Pál-völgyi barlang/ Szemlő-hegyi-barlang) 52
- Tomb of Gül Baba (Gül baba türbeje) 51
- 50 Király Baths (Király fürdő)
- **Buda**
- **Pest**
- Pécel
- Budaörs
- Maglód
- Törökbálint
- 49 Memento Park

7.5 km
4.66 mi

51 TOMB OF GÜL BABA (GÜL BABA TÜRBEJE)

The period under Ottoman rule may still be an uncomfortable chapter in history for many Hungarians. Nevertheless, it was a fruitful period as far as architecture is concerned, with remnants such as the magnificent tomb of Gül Baba, an Ottoman Bektashi (a type of Sufi) *dervish* who came to Hungary with the Ottoman army. After his death in 1541, Sultan Suleiman the Magnificent declared him the patron saint of Buda.

The tomb lies at the foot of Rózsadomb (Rose Hill) and is the most northerly pilgrimage site for Muslims. Completely renovated in 2018, it is a great place to unwind, affording splendid views of Parliament and other city sights, amid smells of roses in spring and summer. The easiest way to get there is from the Margit híd budai hídfő tram stop: walk up Margit körút, Margit utca and Mecset utca to the steps, which lead to the tomb. A more romantic route is from the corner of Frankel Leó út/Török utca: walk up the steep, cobblestoned Gül Baba utca; it's best to leave your flip-flops and high heels back in the hotel. The small *museum (free admission)* on site is open *Tue–Sun 10am–6pm. Mecset utca 14 | District II |* ☐ *B6*

INSIDER TIP
Romantic pilgrimage route

52 PÁLVÖLGYI CAVE & SZEMLŐHEGYI CAVE (PALVÖLGYI BARLANG/ SZEMLŐHEGYI BARLANG)

Time to go underground! These

caves, with their mineral and stalactite formations, are a piece of fascinating nature. They are 800m apart. It is cold in both caves (11°C), so it is a good idea to wear warm clothes as well as stout footwear. *Pálvölgyi Cave (Szépvölgyi út 162 | short.travel/ bud25 | bus 65 from Kolosy tér to the stop Pálvölgyi cseppkőbarlang | ☉ 1 hr)* is the city's longest cave system, measuring 29km in length; 500m of it can be visited as part of a guided tour (no access for children under five or under 115cm tall). The 300m length of *Szemlöhegyi Cave (Pusztaszeri út 35 | short.travel/bud20 | bus 29 from Kolosy tér to Szemlő-hegyi-barlang bus stop | ☉ 40 mins)* are easier to contend with. *Guided tours: Pálvölgyi caves Tue–Sun on the hour from 10.15am–4.15pm; Szemlő-hegyi caves Wed–Mon on the hour from 10am–4pm | admission 2,400 Ft., children 1,900 Ft., combi ticket for both caves 3,900 Ft., children 3,100 Ft. | District II | ▭ 0*

DAY TRIPS

🔢 SZENTENDRE

20km / approx. 50 mins from Deák Ferenc tér (metro, local railway/HÉV)
This lovely town is situated north of Budapest on the Danube Bend. A large number of creative individuals move here at the start of the 20th century. The *Ferenczy Múzeum (Thur–Sun 10am–6pm | Kossuth Lajos utca 5 |*

Dress up warm: there's a chill in the Szemlőhegyi Cave

⏱ 1 hr), between the train station and old town, offers an insight into the history of this artists' colony as well as the artworks of the influential Ferenczy family. The town's seven Orthodox churches were built by Serbian immigrants who had fled from the Ottomans. The narrow streets and the houses built close together are also characteristic features. On the *main square (Fő tér)* you can see a valuable wrought-iron *Memorial Cross* from 1752 and *Blagovescenska Church*, built 1752–54. Only a few steps away is the fine *Margit Kovács Museum (daily 10am–6pm | Vastagh György utca 1 | ⏱ 30 mins)*, which displays the works by the famous ceramicist. There are some great views from *Castle Hill*, which is also the location of Szentendre's oldest church *(Római Katolikus Plébániatemplom). Combi ticket for all the exhibitions in Szentendre costs 1,700 Ft. | muzeum icentrum.hu*

Just 3km northwest of Szentendre is Hungary's largest ethnographic museum, the 🏛 *Skanzen (April–Oct Tue–Sun 9am–5pm | admission 2,600 Ft., families: adults 2,300 Ft., children (6–18) 1,100 Ft | Sztravodai út 75 | skanzen.hu | ⏱ 2 hrs)*. The open-air venue, with several settlements, three churches, a windmill, a historic railway and much more, is an insight into the folk architecture of the Carpathian Basin. *Suburban train/HÉV H5 (trains every 40 mins from Batthyány ter | also boat from Vigadó tér (short.travel/bud28) | ⏱ 0*

INSIDER TIP
A quick stroll through Hungary

🔢 BUDA HILLS (BUDAI-HEGYSÉG)

10km / approx. 40 mins from Deák Ferenc tér to Széchenyi-hegy (metro, tram, cog railway)
Straight from the city into the hills: the *cog railway (Fogaskerekűvasút)* dating from 1874 takes around half an hour to get to the top of *Széchenyi-hegy*. Those of an active disposition can walk up to *János-hegy* (527m), the highest peak of the Buda Hills: first, walk along the *childrens' railway* (see below) to the Normafa stop, from there via Eöt- vös út and Jánoshegyi út up to the top station of the *chairlift (Libegő)* (approx. 45 minutes). The hill is crowned by the stone *Elizabeth Tower*. On clear days visibility can be up to 50 miles!

Those who do not feel like walking the whole way can take the cog railway to the end and then transfer to the 🏛 *childrens' railway* or *Gyermekvasút (May–Aug daily 9am–7pm, Sept–April Tue–Sun 9am–5pm | one-way trip 800 Ft., children 400 Ft. | gyermek vasut.hu/en)* getting out at the Jánoshegy stop. From there, a signposted hiking trail leads upwards (approx. 20 minutes). There is also the *chair lift (Libegö)* that goes up Jánoshegy in 15 minutes from the Zugliget district.

Near the bottom station is the attractive campsite *Ave Natura Camping (campingavenatura.hu/de)* and a place that is meaningful to Germans: in 1989 Imre Kozma, a priest and the former head of the Hungarian Order of Malta, built a camp for people fleeing East Germany near Szarvas Gábor út. *Cog railway (BKK line 60) 5am–11pm, Sun*

Ready for visitors: Gödöllő Palace is Hungary's largest Baroque palace

10am–11pm from the bottom station Városmajor on Szilágyi Erzsébet fasor, can be reached from Széll Kálmán tér by tram 56, 59 or 61 (two stops) | Bottom station chairlift: Zugligeti út | from Nyugati pályaudvar with bus 291 (doesn't go via Széll Kálmán tér) | 🛏 0

55 GÖDÖLLŐ PALACE (GÖDÖLLŐI KIRÁLYI KASTÉLY) ☂

27km / approx 45 minutes HÉV H8 train from Örs vezér tere to Gödöllő's Szabadság tér station

The Austrian Empress and Hungarian Queen Elisabeth (Sisi) often stayed in Gödöllő Palace, east of Budapest. She loved this place, which had been made available to her and her husband, Franz Joseph I, in 1867. Its history began when Prince Antal Grassalkovich made the small village of Gödöllő the centre of his estates in the 18th century. The palace's construction began in around 1740. It is the largest Baroque structure in Hungary. Today Gödöllő is a small town, and the palace and its park are right at the heart of it.

The *Palace Museum (April–Oct daily 10am–6pm, Nov–mid-Jan and mid-Feb–March shorter hours | admission 3,200 Ft., family ticket (2 adults and 3 children) 7,500 Ft. | kiralyikastely.hu | ⏱ 1 hr)* has a 170m² hall, Sisi's chambers and Hungary's only Baroque theatre. Events and concerts are also held at the palace. There is a fine café on the ground floor, or why not enjoy a picnic in the park? 🛏 0

EATING & DRINKING

According to a Hungarian saying, "It's good to eat when you're hungry", so it's best to bring a healthy appetite with you when visiting Budapest.

The city caters for all tastes, with everything from charming, nostalgic coffee houses to modern food temples. By the way, don't take the word "coffee house" too literally: almost all of Budapest's coffee houses and cafés are also restaurants.

You'll find all the venues in this chapter on the pull-out map

crös hot

PA

Paprika: the Hungarian spice of life

Hungarians like to feast to their heart's content. Fried food, lard, cream and sugar feature heavily in every meal, from breakfast to dessert. Many Hungarians would never consider a salad, however satisfying, a complete meal – where's the meat? For hardcore carnivores, we recommend trying quality meat from breeds like the Hungarian *Mangalica* (woolly pig) or *Szürkemarha* (Hungarian grey cattle).

WHERE TO EAT IN BUDAPEST

RÉZMÁL

Margit híd

Duna (Donau)

Margit körút

A. Rotta rakpart

Szehio Gábor rakpart

Carl Lutz rakpart

Teréz körút

📍 Babka ★

VÍZIVÁROS

📍 Igen ★

Attila út

Krisztina körút

VÁR

Id. Antall József rakpart

Friedrich Born rakpart

Bajcsy-Zsilinszky út

LIPÓTVÁROS

Deák Ferenc tér Ⓜ

Alkotás utca

📍 Déryné Bisztró ★

KRISZTINAVÁROS

Erzsébet híd

Kiosk ★ 📍
Napfényes Étterem ★ 📍

Hegyalja út

TABÁN

Henryk Slawik rakpart

BUDA'S CAFÉS & PUBS

Find the best spots along Bartók Béla út, far from the tourist hotspots

Gellérthegy

Szent Gellért tér Ⓜ

NÉMETVÖLGY

Kelet Kávézó és Galéria ★ 📍

Bartók Béla út

Budaörsi út

GELLÉRTHEGY

Móricz Zsigmond körtér Ⓜ

Váci út
Lehel utca
Dózsa György út
Hungária körút

Városliget

ⓑ ÚJLIPÓTVÁROS

JEWISH QUARTER
Eat, drink and be merry!
You'll find everything
you need here

TERÉZVÁROS

Erzsébet körút

Ⓜ Opera

New York Kávéház ★
○

○ Dobrumba ★

○ Bors GasztroBár ★

Rákóczi út

Ⓜ Astoria

BELVÁROS

Ⓜ Kálvin tér

KÁLVIN TÉR
There are plenty of
great places to eat
around the square

Közraktár utca

Duna (Donau)

Soroksári út

TISZTVISELŐTELEP

▲
500 m
546 yd

MARCO POLO HIGHLIGHTS

★ **KELET KÁVÉZÓ ÉS GALÉRIA**
Unpretentious and cosy, whatever the
time of day ➤ p. 68

★ **NEW YORK KÁVÉHÁZ**
Legendary and breathtakingly opulent
➤ p. 70

★ **DÉRYNÉ BISZTRÓ**
Delicious food and a chic ambience
➤ p. 70

★ **KIOSK**
Design meets sophisticated gastronomy
➤ p. 70

★ **BABKA**
Every dish is a hit – and the cocktails will
have you begging for more ➤ p. 72

★ **DOBRUMBA**
An eclectic mix of the Mediterranean
and the Middle East on a plate ➤ p. 72

★ **IGEN**
The best stone-baked pizza in Budapest,
in a stylish setting ➤ p. 73

★ **BORS GASZTROBÁR**
Tiny standing-only restaurant with a
focus on soup ➤ p. 75

★ **NAPFÉNYES ÉTTEREM**
Huge portions of tasty vegan food
➤ p. 76

Hungarians are proud of their culinary traditions, which is why Hungarian cuisine is always a good conversation starter! For a long time, Budapest was quite resistant towards foreign influences, but today change is visibly afoot everywhere. International trends are having an impact, and ambitious Hungarian chefs are discovering lighter versions of their local cuisine. The trend for healthier food is on the rise, especially in the capital. Hungarians are also focusing more and more on slow food, raw food or vegan cooking, with a growing number of young Budapest residents eating more mindfully, focusing on no waste and buying as much as possible locally from the market.

Paprika plays a central role in Hungarian cuisine, both powdered and as a spicy paste (such as *Erős Pista*). The spice gives the dishes a characteristic, but mostly moderate heat. However, just a few of the fresh chilli peppers served on the side or as part of a salad, or as pickled "apple peppers" stuffed with cabbage *(ecetes almapaprika)*, can be very hot indeed.

A pleasing development has taken place in the last decade when it comes to wine. Increasingly, the country is home to passionate winemakers who also know a thing or two about marketing: in fact wine labels are often very stylish, such as the 2018 Sauvignon Blanc from Skizo, the Bodrikutya Cuvée from the Bodri winery or the wines from Dubicz, which even won a high-calibre Red Dot Design Award. Some typical and popular varieties are Kékfrankos, Irsai Olivér, Kadarka and the dessert wine Tokaj Aszú. Hungarian craft beer is also on the rise, internationally too. And you simply can't go without trying the herbal bitter *Unicum* and the fruit brandies *(pálinka)*.

COFFEE HOUSES & CAFÉS

🔟 ANJUNA ICE POPS

Ice pops with a variety of exotic flavours such as mango, masala chai-chocolate and lychee rose, plus *caffè latte* with matcha, açaí bowls and raw cakes made of coconut and raspberry: sounds delicious, right? Anjuna is constantly creating new ice-cream specialities to take away – all made from 100% natural ingredients, with no artificial colours or flavourings, suitable for vegans as well as gluten and lactose-free. *Daily | Sas utca 7 | anjunapops.com | metro 3: Arany János utca | District V | ⅢⅢ d9 | Branches: Lövőház utca 24 | tram 4, 6, 17, 19 Széna tér | District II | ⅢⅢ A7; Pozsonyi út 5 | tram 2, 4, 6 Jászai Mari tér | District XIII | ⅢⅢ C6*

🔟 AUGUSZT

A guaranteed sweet treat. The traditional Auguszt patisserie has been famous for its beautiful cake creations since 1870. While several branches were destroyed during the Second World War, today they have been renovated. Luckily, the old atmosphere, complete with bistro tables, chandeliers and grandparents gossiping over coffee and cake, hasn't been lost. Organic milk, butter and eggs are

Step back in time to a more glamorous age at Centrál Kávéház

used here, and the excellent quality of the ingredients turns the cakes and ice-creams into exquisite treats that can be enjoyed at the bistro tables. *Tue–Sat* | *Kossuth Lajos utca 14–16* | *auguszt.hu* | *metro 3: Ferenciek tere* | *District V* | ᵭ d10 | *Branches: Fény utca 8* | *metro 2 Széll Kálmán tér* | *District II* | ᵭ A7; *Sasadi út 190 (closed Mon/Tue)* | *tram 59 or bus 8E Márton Áron tér* | *District XI* | ᵭ 0

ᴇ CENTRÁL KÁVÉHÁZ

Like something out of a film, this coffee house dating from 1887 just oozes prestige and elegance. Black-and-white pictures on the walls pay tribute to the intellectuals and actors who used to come and go here, including poet Endre Ady.

Order a "Pest coffee" (*pesti kávé*, a house speciality) and a quark

INSIDER TIP
Take a break

cheese slice with apricot jam *(Rákóczi túrós)*, while you decide where to head next. *Daily* | *Károlyi Mihály utca 9* | *centralkavehaz.hu* | *metro 3: Ferenciek tere* | *District V* | ᵭ d10

ᴇ CSÉSZÉNYI KÁVÉZÓ ÉS PÖRKÖLŐ

A place that's not known to many, the Csészényi in Buda is a delightfully cosy café with mouth-watering coffee and cake specialties, all made from natural ingredients without any additives. One of the walls is covered with old hand-held coffee grinders and older locals like coming here to read their newspapers in peace. A good

Stunning splendour: New York Kávéház

time is guaranteed! *Daily | Krisztina körút 34 | cseszenyi.hu | tram 17, 19, 41, 56 Krisztina tér | bus 105 |* District I | ⌁ a9

◪ CAFÉ GERBEAUD

Admittedly, the Gerbeaud is over-priced, but it's worth it

INSIDER TIP
Pockets of cheese

for its mouth-watering cream cheese-filled pastries alone. The French pastry chef and chocolatier Emil Gerbeaud took over the legendary coffee house from his Hungarian colleague in 1884. The traditional establishment oozes nostalgic charm from the interior and exterior design to the enchanting old-school waiters. No wonder that a 15% tip is automatically added to the total amount on the bill. *Daily | Vörösmarty tér 7–8 | gerbeaud.hu | metro 1: Vörösmarty tér |* District V | ⌁ d9

◨ JEDERMANN

Jedermann is the little brother of the neighbouring Goethe Institute, and is relaxed yet sophisticated. Owner Hans van Vliet is an amateur jazz musician and there is often live jazz and folk music in the evenings. After breakfast, the relaxed café, situated at the bottom end of Ráday utca, offers cheap lunch menus. There's a small, hidden court-

INSIDER TIP
Al fresco dining

yard at the back where you can eat and drink in the summer. *Daily | Ráday utca 58 | jedermann.hu | tram 2, 4, 6 Boráros tér |* District IX | ⌁ E12

◧ KELET KÁVÉZÓ ÉS GALÉRIA ★

A newish café that nevertheless offers a charm and cosiness that's lacking in some of the more expensive, famous coffee houses. Plus, it's truly multifunctional: the bookshelves on the

Today's specials

Starters

PADLIZSÁNKRÉM
Mashed aubergine with flatbread and fresh vegetables

VELŐS PIRÍTÓS
Toasted bread with bone marrow

Soups

GULYÁSLEVES
Goulash soup

SZEGEDI HALÁSZLÉ
Szeged-style fish soup

FOKHAGYMALEVES
Creamy garlic soup with croutons

Mains

VÖRÖSBOROS MARHAPÖRKÖLT SZTRAPACSKÁVAL
Red wine *pörkölt* (something between a stew and a goulash) with beef and potato noodles

PAPRIKÁS CSIRKE GALUSKÁVAL
Paprika chicken with egg noodles

VEGETÁRIÁNUS TÁL
Fried vegetarian platter with cheese, cauliflower, mushrooms and courgettes, served with French fries or rice

TEJFÖLÖS UBROKASALÁTA
Pickled cucumber salad with sour cream

VEGYES SAVANYÚSÁGOK
Selection of pickled vegetables (white cabbage, peppers, cucumbers)

Desserts

SOMLÓI GALUSKA
Hungarian chocolate trifle; sponge with chocolate sauce and whipped cream

GUNDEL PALACSINTA
A pancake dish developed at the storied Gundel restaurant, topped with walnuts, chocolate sauce and whipped cream

GESZTENYEPÜRÉ
Chestnut dessert with whipped cream

Drinks

HÁZI LIMONÁDÉ
Homemade lemonade

SZÖRPÖK
Fruit syrup spritzer: raspberry (*málna*), elderberry (*bodza*) or rosehip (*csipkebogyó*)

PÁLINKA
Fruit schnapps (apricot, plum or pear)

wall are lined with books to browse (some in English), and there is plenty of breakfast, main meals, coffee, cake and beer to go round. Regular cultural events, occasionally in English. *Daily | Bartók Béla út 29 | FB: keletkavezo | tram 17, 19, 41, 47, 48, 49, 56, 56A Gárdonyi tér | District XI | ▥ D12*

8 NEW YORK KÁVÉHÁZ ★ ⚑

The neo-Baroque opulence of this legendary café, which styles itself as the most beautiful in the world, is breath-taking. Other cafés are cosier, but to have a coffee in such magnificent surroundings, or to enjoy a piece of cake or a fruit shake, are experiences not to be missed! *Daily | Erzsébet körút 9–11 | newyorkcafe.hu | metro 2: Blaha Lujza tér | tram 4, 6 | District VII | ▥ F9*

RESTAURANTS €€€

9 COSTES DOWNTOWN

Michelin-star cuisine in a casual setting? Yes, really! Breakfast, lunch and dinner are all prepared in the open-plan kitchen and served to guests as they sit amid contemporary works of art. This restaurant is a spin-off of Costes in the Ráday utca – the first Budapest restaurant to be awarded a Michelin star. *Closed Sun/Mon | Vigyázó Ferenc utca 5 | tel. 20 926 7837 | costesdowntown.hu | tram 2 Széchenyi István tér | District V | ▥ C9*

10 DÉRYNÉ BISZTRÓ ★ ⚑

This bistro takes good food, service and design seriously without being too snobbish. The menu is low key, but

everything is prepared to perfection and there is a great brunch served on Sundays between 9am and 4pm. By the way, the cosy cabin in front of the restaurant is used for baking the delicious homemade Déryné bread. Try it for yourself. *Daily | Krisztina tér 3 | tel. 1 225 1407 | bistroderyne.com | tram 17, 19, 41, 56 | bus 105 | District I | ▥ a9*

INSIDER TIP
Delicious bread to take away

11 ÉS BISZTRÓ

In Hungarian, *és* means "and", and – true to its word – this bistro is also a steakhouse and luxury restaurant, as well as a pub and wine bar. The place manages to combine a relaxing atmosphere with extremely high-quality food. Order the hay steak if you want the ultimate steak experience – Austrian beef which has been wrapped in hay and herbs and stored for three weeks. A pleasure for all the senses. *Daily | Deák Ferenc utca 12–14 | tel. 1 429 3990 | esbisztro.hu | metro 1, 2, 3: Deák Ferenc tér | tram 47, 48, 49 | District V | ▥ d9*

12 KIOSK ★

Two reasons to stop by: the in-house pastry shop and the homemade ice cream. But there are plenty of other reasons, too, and if you enjoy interior design, there's plenty to admire as you eat. The menu is split into classics and Hungarian dishes, but it's also worth taking a look at the cocktail menu. Lovely view from the large terrace outside. Plus, you can book easily online. *Daily | Március 15. tér 4 |*

Michelin-starred bistro or art venue? Costes Downtown is relaxed and stylish

tel. 70 311 1969 | kiosk-budapest.hu | tram 2 Március 15. tér | metro 3: Ferenciek tere | District V | □□ d10

13 MÁK BISTRO

The Mák team are on a mission to free top gastronomy from formalities, making it fun for everyone. The chefs here value clean eating as much as the enjoyment and sheer pleasure of eating. The menu is never without a dish with poppy seeds *(mák)*. You can book online. *Closed Sun/Mon | Vigyázó Ferenc utca 4 | tel. 30 723 9383 | mak.hu | tram 2 Széchenyi István tér | District V | □□ c9*

14 STAND RESTAURANT

Stand is home to a team of young, progressive chefs cooking up Hungarian and fusion cuisine – see and taste the results for yourself on your plate! The place has won awards and received its first Michelin star in 2019, just nine months after opening. Last entry at 8pm. *Closed Sun/Mon | Székely Mihály utca 2 | tel. 30 785 9139 | standrestaurant.hu | metro 1: Opera | District VI | □□ e9*

15 TOKIO

Sushi, pad thai and black sesame ice cream: if you like Asian fusion cuisine and culinary authenticity in a stylish ambience, you'll enjoy Tokio. The chefs always add that little something extra to every dish. But you're also in the right place if you're looking to transition from dinner to nightlife. The sake selection is impressive. Book online.

Daily | Széchenyi István tér 7–8 | tel. 70 333 2176 | tokiobudapest.com | Strassenbahn 2 Széchenyi István tér | District V | ꕹ c9

RESTAURANTS €€

16 BABKA ⭐

Babka is nicely furnished and joyfully cosy, and in summer you can sit on the terrace and watch the comings and goings on Pozsonyi út. You'll also find what really matters here: good food. The cuisine is inspired by Jewish Middle Eastern cuisine, with a healthy dash of Hungarian flavour. There are also delicious cocktails and friendly, professional wine advice – great fun all round. Booking essential. Closed lunch Tue/Wed | Pozsonyi út 3 | tel. 1 789 9672 | FB: babkabudapest | tram 2, 4, 6 Jászai Mari tér | District XIII | ꕹ C6

17 DOBRUMBA ⭐

Dobrumba is what Budapest has been waiting for: this hip establishment is geared towards young people and serves a delicious blend of flavours hailing from the Middle East and the Mediterranean. Fans of couscous and lamb come on in! Reservations are essential (you can book online). Daily | Dob Utca 5 | tel. 30 194 0049 | dobrumba.hu | metro 2: Astoria | tram 47, 48, 49 | District VII | ꕹ e9

18 FAUSTO'S

This excellent restaurant, right next to the synagogue in Dohány utca, can be relied on for its Mediterranean and contemporary Italian cuisine. Owner Fausto di Vora has been gastronomically active in Budapest for more than 20 years. Closed Sun/Mon | Dohány utca 5 | tel. 30 589 1813 | fausto.hu | metro 2: Astoria | tram 47, 48, 49 | District VII | ꕹ e10

19 FRANZISKA

Breakfast, brunch, lunch, coffee, cake. Even just grabbing a bite to eat in between meals is a lovely experience here. Not only is the interior beautiful, but the service is attentive and the food absolutely delicious. Owner Franciska Horváth puts an emphasis on seasonal and healthy ingredients and always has an eye on current trends, with the likes of smoothies and bowls. Closed Mon | Iskola utca 29 | franziska.hu | metro 2 Batthyány tér | tram 19, 41 | District I | ꕹ b8

20 GERLÓCZY

A touch of Paris in Budapest – the Gerlóczy is a friendly café/restaurant with a wonderful terrace, located in a small square in the city centre. Breakfast is worth the walk and in the evening you can dine pleasantly under colourful lanterns. You can also rent comfortable rooms on the upper floors. Daily | Gerlóczy utca 1 | tel. 1 501 4000 | gerloczy.hu | metro 2: Astoria | tram 47, 48, 49 | District V | ꕹ d10

21 GETTÓ GULYÁS

Some of the walls at Gettó Gulyás are covered with transparent corrugated plastic stuffed with straw, making for an original look. Old Hungarian pictures and wine bottles complete the setting. Anyway, on to the food:

Café-restaurant Gerlóczy, with its inviting terrace, is a welcome pit-stop in the city centre

the dishes are all modern interpretations of classic Hungarian recipes. As the name suggests, the restaurant specialises in goulash, as well as stews and *pörkölt* (something between a stew and a goulash). Plenty for vegetarians too. *Daily | Wesselényi utca 18 | tel. 20 376 4480 | FB: gettogulyas | metro 2 Astoria | tram 47, 48, 49 | District VII | ㎝ e9*

㉒ IGEN ★

A big fat "yes" (*igen*) to pizza! Especially when it's cooked in a stone oven. This restaurant on the Buda side serves southern Italian-style pizza – thin dough, crispy crust and rich in flavour. Vegan, vegetarian, gluten-free and wholemeal options are available. Tip: why not order a limoncello spritz to go with it? *Daily | Margit körút 60 | FB: igenitalia | tram 4, 6 Mechwart liget | District II | ㎝ A7*

㉓ KŐLEVES VENDÉGLŐ

The basic ingredients here – pasta, bread, preserves and sauces – are homemade and dishes are made with seasonal produce. The atmospheric beer garden next door (open in summer only) also serves barbecued food. Located in the centre of the Jewish Quarter, the restaurant is housed in the premises of an old kosher meat plant – and, in keeping with tradition, there are no pork dishes on the menu. *Closed Sun | Kazinczy utca 41 | tel. 20 213 5999 | kolevesvendeglo.hu | metro 2: Astoria | tram 47, 48, 49 | District VII | ㎝ e9*

Head to Menza on Liszt Ferenc tér for retro décor and delicious pancakes

24 KÖNYVBÁR
Dishes inspired by books, served in a book-lined space with the cosy atmosphere of a reading room or library. The cuisine is international, the restaurant bright and cosy. An absolute must for fans of literature and the big screen! *Closed Sun | Dob utca 45 | tel. 20 922 7027 | konyvbar.hu | tram 4, 6 Király utca | District VII | ⚏ e9*

25 MENZA
Menza is decorated in a trendy, retro 1970s and 1980s style. The menu lists many soups and salads as well as main dishes ranging from *penne* to *lángos* (traditional Hungarian deep-fried flatbread) and duck. The *palacsinta* (pancakes) with quark covered in vanilla sauce and meringue are delicious. Inexpensive daily specials. *Daily | Liszt Ferenc tér 2 | tel. 30 145 4242 | menzaetterem.hu | metro 1: Oktogon | District VI | ⚏ E8*

26 SPINOZA
In the heart of the old Jewish Quarter, the Spinoza is a successful crossover of simple restaurant, stylish café and event venue for klezmer music evenings (Fridays from 7pm). Other evenings regularly feature piano music. *Closed Tue/Wed | Dob utca 15 | tel. 1 413 7488 | FB: spinozarestaurant | metro 1, 2, 3 Deák Ferenc tér | tram 47, 48, 49 | District VII | ⚏ e9*

27 STÉG
Do you have a weakness for fish? Or just fancy a bowl of *halászlé* (fish

soup)? Then Stég is the ideal place – a small, tastefully decorated restaurant serving classics such as fish and chips.

INSIDER TIP
Fish cooked Hungarian-style
However, it's best to try the *keszeg*, a type of carp and a Hungarian speciality, paired with one of the excellent Hungarian wines from Sauska and Dúzsi Tamás. For those who don't eat fish, the restaurant also serves traditional *lángos* flatbreads. A set meal is available every weekday. *Daily | Gozsdu Court, Dob utca 16 | tel. 70 420 3332 | stegfood. hu | metro 1, 2, 3: Deák Ferenc tér | tram 47, 48, 49 | District VII | ⌂ e9*

RESTAURANTS €

㉘ BÉLA

The place may look thrown together, but there's a concept behind the eclecticism, and the atmosphere is cosy yet modern. Béla is perfect for different moods and occasions, whether you fancy a coffee and quick bite or beer and a hearty dinner. Choose between a table in the cosy interior or outside on the terrace if the weather is fine. *Daily | Bartók Béla út 23 | tel. 70 590 7974 | belabudapest. com | tram 17, 19, 41, 47, 48, 49, 56 Gárdonyi tér | District XI | ⌂ D12*

㉙ BORS GASZTRÓBÁR ★

In Hungary, there's a saying that "the pepper is small yet spicy". It's roughly equivalent to "small things come in small packages" and is a fitting description for this street-food bar cum bistro. The chefs

György Rethling and Tamás Lipher create soups to take away, as

well as gourmet grilled baguettes, pasta dishes with a twist, and delicious juices and desserts. Judging by the interior design and background music, they obviously share a passion for Star Wars and rap music. A tiny yet delightful establishment. *Daily | Kazinczy utca 10 | tel. 30 698 9075 | FB: BorsGasztroBar | metro 2: Astoria | tram 47, 48, 49 | District VII | ⌂ e9*

㉚ FRICI PAPA KIFŐZDÉJE

If you fancy hearty, inexpensive Hungarian dishes and aren't scared by a slightly higher fat content, then "Papa Frici's Cookshop" is the place for you – a legendary favourite among Budapest locals. Daily specials also on the menu. *Closed Sun | Király utca 55 | fricipapa.hu | tram 4, 6 Király utca/ Erzsébet körút | District VII | ⌂ E8*

㉛ FRUCCOLA

Fresh fruit juices and salads, crunchy croissants for breakfast and cheap lunches – the Fruccola is a healthy contrast to typical Hungarian food, which can be on the heavy side. You can **INSIDER TIP**
Herbivores delight!
assemble your own salad, and there is a choice of daily meals and desserts. Ideal for vegetarians and vegans. *Closed Sun | Arany János utca 32 | fruccola.hu | metro 3: Arany János utca) | District V | ⌂ D8. Branch: MOM Park | Lisszabon sétány | tram 17, 41, 61 Csörsz utca | District XII | ⌂ A10*

32 HUMMUS BAR

You like falafel and hummus? Then you'll enjoy eating in the Hummus Bar. The shakshuka is especially tasty, too! There are several branches and takeaway is also available. *Daily | Nagymező utca 10 | tel. 70 609 9522 | hummusbar.hu | metro 1: Opera | District VI | E8 | Branch: Október 6 utca 19 | tel. 70 380 1859 | metro 3: Arany János utca) | District V | D8*

33 KABUL BÜFÉ

This small, simple bistro serves original Afghan dishes. The owner is a friendly gentleman who is more than happy to explain the small but fine selection of food on display. There's always a vegetarian option. *Closed Sun, otherwise 10am–8pm | Népszínház utca 27 | FB: kabulbufe | metro 2 Blaha Lujza tér | District VIII | F10*

34 NAPFÉNYES ÉTTEREM ★

Napfény translates as "sunshine", a perfect word to sum up this vegan restaurant in meat-loving Budapest. The enormous portions are enough to fill the most passionate carnivores, and are made using organic ingredients. The delicious food ranges from Hungarian to international dishes and you can put together your own salads at the salad bar. There is also a set meal served every weekday. No alcoholic or caffeine beverages are served. *Daily | Ferenciek tere 2 | tel. 20 311 0313 | napfenyesetterem.hu | metro 3 Ferenciek tere | District V | d10*

35 ORIENTAL SOUP HOUSE

Budapest is awash with Asian and especially Chinese restaurants – but be careful, because the food in many of them is not authentic (or even edible in some cases). On the other hand, the Oriental Soup House serves

VEGETARIAN HEAVEN

Goulash can be animal-friendly! Vegan goulash restaurants are popping up like mushrooms all over Budapest. The city also offers a great selection of meat-free street food. You'll find tasty treats at *Las Vegan's food trucks (Street Food Karavan | Kazinczy utca 18 | las vegans.eu | District VII | e9 | promenade next to the Allee shopping centre | District XI | C13)*, at *Epoch Vegan Burger (Királyi Pál utca 20 | epochburger.hu | District V | e11)* or *Vegan Love (Bartók Béla út 9 | veganlove.hu | District XI | D12)*.

If you can't make your mind up what you fancy eating, head to *Vegan Garden (Király utca 8-10 | vegangardenbudapest.com | District VII | d9)*, which has a long and varied menu.

Despite the wide choice of vegetarian food available in Budapest, don't expect everyone to know what "vegan" means – Hungary's older generation, especially, tend not to regard chicken or fish as real "meat".

Stroll from stall to stall in food heaven: Street Food Karaván

genuine Asian dishes such as pho in hearty portions. Good vegetarian and vegan options available. Both the service and interior design are appealing. A quick tip: if you can avoid it, try not to sit upstairs on the gallery – annoyingly, all the steam from the open kitchen rises up there. Cash only. *Daily | Balzac utca 35 | tel. 70 617 3535 | FB: orientalsouphouse | tram 4, 6 Jászai Mari tér* | District XIII | *D6*

36 STREET FOOD KARAVÁN

Looking to grab a filling bite to eat? Then head to *Street Food Karaván*, an outdoor food court with white pebbles and long benches. It houses a dozen or so food trucks selling a variety of appetising snacks from *lángos, kürtőskalács* and hamburgers, as well as craft beer and homemade lemonade. A great, friendly place. *Daily | Kazinczy utca 18 | FB: streetfood karavan | metro 2 Astoria* | District VII | *e9*

37 WHY NOT BISTRO

You'll leave here feeling full and satisfied, that's for sure! The bistro and the nearby *Why Not Cafe and Bar (Belgrád rakpart 3–4)*, with regular karaoke and drag shows, are without advertising this too strongly to the outside world, places that are open to everyone, including and especially people from the LGBTQ+ community. The atmosphere is relaxed, while the small terrace and view of the Liberty Statue on Gellért Hill from the bistro round off the experience. *Daily | Belgrád rakpart 18 | whynotbistro.hu | tram 2 Március 15. tér* | District V | *d11*

SHOPPING

Good news for everyone mad about shopping and souvenir-hunting: shops are as much a part of Budapest culture as its coffee houses. Run-of-the-mill chain stores, out-of-the-ordinary art shops or buzzing markets – the choice is entirely up to you.

The pedestrian zone Váci utca in Pest is packed with shops selling everything from international and Hungarian fashion and beauty brands to porcelain, folklore items and classic kitschy souvenirs. The southern section (Szabad sajtó út to Fővám tér) is quieter and you

You'll find all the venues in this chapter on the pull-out map 🗺

Find all sorts of produce in the Central Market Hall

will find smaller shops with Hungarian products here. Király utca, which runs parallel to Andrássy út, is a top address for design fans, with its furniture and homewares stores. The 4.5-km Grand Boulevard (Nagykörút) between Margaret Bridge and Petőfi Bridge still has old-fashioned shops (selling, for example, fabrics by the metre). However, these are gradually disappearing. The young, in particular, are drawn to modern shopping centres with their range of fashion outlets, fast-food restaurants, gyms and cinemas.

WHERE TO SHOP IN BUDAPEST

RÉZMÁL

Wamp Design Market (Millenáris) ★

ORSZÁGÚT

VÍZIVÁROS

Margit híd

Margit körút

A. Rotta rakpart

Duna (Donau)

VÁCI UTC

The usual fashic
suspects side by sic
with souveni

Attila út

Krisztina körút

VÁR

Friedrich Born rakpart

MARCO POLO HIGHLIGHTS

★ **MASSOLIT BOOKS & CAFÉ**
A must for bookworms and coffee addicts
➤ p. 83

★ **FOLKART KÉZMŰVESHÁZ**
Folk art in the heart of the city centre
➤ p. 85

★ **WAMP DESIGN MARKET**
All sorts of handicrafts, from clothes and
jewellery to tableware ➤ p. 85

★ **CENTRAL MARKET HALL**
Paprika and salami under steel and glass
➤ p. 85

★ **HUMANA VINTAGE BUTIK**
Well-stocked second-hand shop with a
great clothes selection ➤ p. 87

★ **PREZENT**
Regional souvenirs with a green backstory
➤ p. 87

★ **RETROCK**
Cool and crazy clothing ➤ p. 88

★ **HEREND PORCELAIN**
Hungary's finest porcelain ➤ p. 88

★ **TISZA CIPŐ**
Shoes made in Hungary that manage to
be both comfy and stylish ➤ p. 89

★ **BORTÁRSASÁG**
Amazing selection of Hungarian wines
➤ p. 89

ÚJLIPÓTVÁROS

Carl Lutz rakpart

Teréz körút

Lehel utca

Váci út

ANDRÁSSY ÚT

Chic designer stores:
the place to shop

Andrássy út

📍 Bortársaság ★

Oktogon

TERÉZVÁROS

LIPÓTVÁROS

Bajcsy-Zsilinszky út

Opera

📍 Herend Porcelain ★

Bajcsy-Zsilinszky út

Herend Porcelain
(József Nádor tér) ★

Massolit Books
& Café ★

📍 Retrock ★

Wamp Design Market ★

Vörösmarty tér

Folkart Kézműveshaz ★

📍 Humana Vintage Butik ★
📍 Tisza Cipő ★

JEWISH QUARTER

Hip, handmade and
repurposed items from
Budapest's young
designers

Rákóczi út

📍 Prezent ★

BELVÁROS

Üllői út

Henryk Slawik rakpart

Duna (Dunaj)

Gellérthegy

📍 Central Market Hall
(Központi Vásárcsarnok) ★

400 m
437 yd

Hungarian food specialities are always a popular souvenir. The most popular and tasty items include spicy Hungarian salami or smoked sausage *(szalámi, kolbász)*, marzipan (for example, from Szamos), wine *(bor)*, fruit brandy *(pálinka)* and herbal liqueur *(unicum)*. Other favourites to take back home include ceramics and porcelain, (Zsolnay and Herend are popular brands) and hand-embroidered tablecloths (especially those in Matyó style). Young designers are reinventing traditional patterns to create new fashion styles. Casual streetwear like you'll find in the BP Shop (p. 86) is also popular – T-shirts with the inscription "Buda fckn Pest" are evrywhere. Falk Miksa utca is known as Budapest's antiques row and is lined with renowned antique shops and art galleries.

WHERE TO START?

Váci utca *(🚇 D9-10)* and its side streets are a shopping mecca. International fashion and shoe labels are represented here, as are small, independent Hungarian shops. **Vörösmarty tér** is home to new shopping centres; if you turn right you will find yourself in the small **Deák Ferenc utca** ("Fashion Street"). Looking for international luxury brands? Then explore the boulevard **Andrássy út** *(🚇 D–F 7–9)*. The largest shopping centre is the **Westend City Center** *(🚇 D–E 6–7)*.

ANTIQUES & COLLECTIBLES

1 NAGYHÁZI

Jewellery, antique furniture, carpets, porcelain, paintings and more: this family-owned auction house is always worth a visit. *Balaton utca 8 | corner of Falk Miksa utca | nagyhazi.hu | tram 2, 4, 6 Jászai Mari tér | District V | 🚇 C7*

2 TABÁNI GARÁZSVÁSÁR

It's no coincidence that this antiques store is called "Garage Sale" in Hungarian: unlike the other, more high-end antique dealers on the Falk Miksa utca, Zsolt Rédei's store is lined with shelves full of bric-a-brac. Maci is the name of the owner's cute dog that usually lies sprawled out in the entrance – just climb over him! *Döbrentei utca l | tram 19, 41 Várkert Bazár | District I | 🚇 c10*

BOOKS & MUSIC

3 BODRY

While Budapest's district VIII once suffered from a rather murky reputation, shops like Bodry are proof that the neighbourhood is now very cool! The shop sells mostly vinyl records, both old and new. There is music from all over the world and from the latest from Hungarian punk bands, as well as underground 'zines and all kinds of handmade items by young designers. Happy browsing! *Bródy Sándor utca 25 | FB: bodry.sandor | tram 4, 6 Rákóczi tér | District VIII | 🚇 F10*

4 COMIC LIBRARY IN NEM ADOM FEL KÁVÉZÓ

Back in 2018, two young comic book enthusiasts, who also researched comics at university, opened this comic book library *(Képregénykönyvtár)*. Head to their Facebook page for the catalogue of all available comics (including many in English) in the form of a spreadsheet linked to the Facebook page. But the big draw is also its location: the *Nem Adom Fel* (Never Give Up) café was founded by a group of disabled people who also run the place. A great initiative all round. *Magdolna utca 1 | FB: kepregeny konyvtar | tram 4, 6 Harminckettesek tere | District VIII | ☐ G10*

INSIDER TIP
Comics and a coffee shop!

5 MASSOLIT BOOKS & CAFÉ ★ ☂

Coffee, cakes and snacks – but above all books – are available in this endearing cultural café, which you'll fall in love with as soon as you enter. The foreign-language books are aimed at an open and toler-ant crowd, with themes such as progressive politics, feminism and Jewish studies, rather than mainstream literature. There's a cosy garden and frequent public readings, film showings and acoustic concerts. *Nagy Diófa utca 30 | FB: MassolitBudapest | metro 2: Blaha Lujza tér | District VII | ☐ e9*

6 MÉDIA PONT A LEMEZBOLT

This tiny second-hand record shop certainly isn't shy: its outside has been painted red and the inside is

Shop in style on Andrássy út

decorated with vinyl and record covers. You'll usually be greeted by the wonderfully relaxed owner István and his three miniature dogs Csipi, Gizmo and Drazsé. The record shop is piled high with vinyl and CDs – from Nat King Cole to Hungarian fairy tales and Bananarama. Best pay it a visit now before it's overrun with hipsters! *Hollán Ernő utca 18 | FB: Média-Pont-a-lemezbolt | tram 2, 4, 6 Jászai Mari tér | District XIII | ☐ D6*

Choose paprika over melons if you're souvenir shopping at the Central Market Hall

SHOPPING CENTRES

7 MOM PARK

Modern shopping centre that attracts an upmarket crowd of Buda locals with cash-filled wallets. The lower level has some great delicatessens; among them is the Bortársaság wine store. The pretty *Pink Cinema* on the top floor shows good films, usually not dubbed. *Alkotás út 53/corner of Csörsz utca | mompark. hu | tram 17, 61 Csörsz utca | District XII | ⌂ A10*

> **INSIDER TIP**
> **With or without subtitles**

8 WESTEND CITY CENTER

This bright temple of consumerism has countless shops selling everything from fashion to technology. There are touchscreens dotted around the centre providing information on where shops are located. The lower floor is a food court hosting all types of fast-food outlets (the delicious Indian-Pakistani *Kohinoor* is particularly recommended), while the top floor houses *Cinema City*, where English-language films are often shown. The rooftop terrace has an ice rink in winter. *Váci út 1–3, near Western Station | westend.hu | metro 3: Nyugati pályaudvar | District VI | ⌂ D–E 6–7*

ARTS & CRAFTS

9 APACUKA CERAMICS

For Judit Neuvirth and Gábor Födő, the couple behind this ceramics studio, this place really is a dream come true. They offer pottery workshops (including some in English) or you can buy beautiful ceramics inspired by shapes and patterns from Hungarian folklore. *Bajnok utca 30 | apacuka ceramics.hu | metro 1 Kodály körönd | District VI | ⊞ E7*

🔟 FOLKART KÉZMŰVESHÁZ ★

This store in the city centre sells a stunning collection of Hungarian arts and crafts made of wood, fabrics and ceramic, whether carved, embroidered or painted. *Régiposta utca 12 | folkartkezmuveshaz.hu | metro 1: Vörösmarty tér | District V | ⊞ d10*

MARKETS & DELICATESSENS

🔟 CULINARIS

A delicatessen with delicacies from all over the world. If you want to have a picnic in the neighbouring Olympia Park, for example, you could find fine *antipasti*, rolls or cheese here. *Balassi Bálint utca 7 | culinaris.hu | tram 2 Országház/látogatóközpont | District V | ⊞ C7 | Branch: Perc utca 8 | bus 9 Tímár utca) | District III | ⊞ C3*

🔟 FÉNY UTCAI PIAC

The market along the Fény utca is worth visiting for its authentic Hungarian market atmosphere and delicious specialities. Here, friendly old ladies sell vegetables grown in their own gardens.

INSIDER TIP
Hungarian snacks

You will also find the traditional Mangalica smoked sausage and the *lángos* stall on the first floor is legendary (even if its

appearance is not up to much). The stalls usually open at 6am and close around 2pm. *Lövőház utca 12 | tram 4, 6, 17, 19 Széna tér | District II | ⊞ A7*

🔟 WAMP DESIGN MARKET ★

Earrings upcycled from buttons and bags from rubber bike tyres, hand-painted crockery and hand-sewn ties – the list is never ending... This market, featuring the work of young Hungarian designers and specialising in DIY and upcycled products, is unique. It is usually held on the first Sunday of the month from April to September at the Várkert Bazaar (Castle Garden Bazaar), and otherwise indoors in the *Millenáris* cultural and recreational centre. *Várkert Bazár: tram 19, 41 Várkert Bazár | District V | ⊞ c10 | Millenáris: Kis Rókus utca 16–20 | tram 4, 6, 17, 19 Széna tér | wamp.hu/en | District II | ⊞ A7*

🔟 CENTRAL MARKET HALL (KÖZPONTI VÁSÁRCSARNOK) ★ ☂

You will get the best view of the 150m-long market hall with its two aisles from one of the transverse corridors on the top floor. Designed by Samu Pecz, this beautiful building was radically modern at the time it was built in 1890. Even though almost no visitor to Budapest leaves without seeing it, it is not an establishment for tourists, but one of the country's most important markets. Whether it's fruit, vegetables, meat or fish, this place sells everything you could want. On the first floor, you can choose between savoury or sweet *lángos* (often with sour cream and cheese) – both absolutely delicious. If you're looking for souvenirs, you can buy them here too. Haggle! *Vámház körút 1–3 | metro 4: Fővám tér | tram 2, 47, 47B, 48, 49 | District IX | ⊞ e11*

FASHION & DESIGN

🔢 BP SHOP

The cool young guys behind the fashion label BP are so proud of their home city, they print it large on their ultra-casual, hip-hop style T-shirts, caps, hoodies and shoes. New collections for both men and women on a regular basis – perfect as a cool souvenir! *Hercegprímás utca 6 (also open Sun) | bpshop.hu | metro 1: Bajcsy-Zsilinszky út | District V | ⊞ d9*

> **INSIDER TIP**
> **Super streetwear!**

🔢 DEÁK FERENC UTCA

This road is also known as "Fashion Street" because a large number of clothing brands have opened shops here, such as Hugo Boss, Prada, Tommy Hilfiger and Dolce & Gabbana. *Deák Ferenc utca | metro 1, 2, 3: Deák Ferenc tér | District V | ⊞ d9*

🔢 ÉKES KESZTYŰ

Small but mighty: Ékes Kesztyű is Hungarian for "pretty glove". This little, unassuming shop in the city centre of Pest sells handmade gloves and hats manufactured by the third generation of a local family that takes its craft very seriously. *Régiposta utca 14 | FB: ekeskesztyu | metro 1: Vörösmarty tér | District V | ⊞ d10*

Eco shopping – Printa sells sustainable design, from T-shirts to bags

18 HUMANA VINTAGE BUTIK ⭐

Looking for something out of the ordinary rather than off the peg but don't want to trek around the shops? Whatever your style, this compact vintage spin-off store from the Humana chain of second-hand shops is for you. Expect to be asked where you got your amazing clothes from when you get back home. *Károly körút 8 | FB: humanavintagebutik | metro 2: Astoria | tram 47, 49 | District V | 🕮 e10*

19 LOVEBUG VINTAGE

Bright and bursting to the brim, this shop, housed in an old apartment, sells everything from second-hand clothes to the latest trends. To get in, you first have to ring the bell outside, then turn left once you're in the building. Cool leather jackets, funny printed shirts or old Hungarian records. Whatever you're looking for, you can easily spend hours browsing this vintage treasure trove. Owner Violetta Kertész picks out absolutely everything herself. *Margit körút 62, bell no. 11 | instagram.com/lovebug vintagebudapest | tram 4, 6, 17 Mechwart liget | District II | 🕮 A7*

INSIDER TIP
Vintage everything

20 MONO ART & DESIGN

Mono was one of the first stores in Budapest to sell fashion designed by young Hungarians. The choice is amazing (even for men) and is continuously updated; there is something here to suit everyone's wallet. The shop also has an interesting collection of jewellery and accessories. *Kossuth Lajos utca 20 | FB: monoartanddesign | metro 2: Astoria | tram 47, 48, 49 | District V | 🕮 d10*

INSIDER TIP
A great place for gifts!

21 NANUSHKA STORE & CAFÉ

"Nanuska" was the nickname of fashion designer Szandra Sándor when she was a young girl. Nobody would have thought back then that she would go on to create her own fashion label sold in stores from New York to Hong Kong. Her designs are up-to-the-minute yet timeless, playful and minimalistic. *Bécsi utca 3 | nanushka.com | metro 1: Vörösmarty tér | District V | 🕮 d9*

22 PREZENT ⭐

If you'd love to be an environmentalist but care too much about shopping, then this is the store for you. Sustainability is the number one priority here: everything – from postcards and children's toys to jam – comes from Hungary and lots of the products are organic or upcycled. Buy great souvenirs with a clear conscience. *Döbrentei utca 16 | FB: prezent budapest | tram 19 | bus 8E, 108E, 110, 112 Döbrentei tér | District I | 🕮 c10*

23 PRINTA

A creative centre for environmentally conscious design, exhibitions, art and textile prints. You can buy clothes such as T-shirts, as well as bags, lampshades and jewellery, from 17 designers. The coffee in the café comes from a fair trade project. The centre is closed on Sunday, *Rumbach Sebestyén utca 10a | printa.hu | metro 1, 2, 3: Deák Ferenc tér | District VII | 🕮 e9*

24 RETROCK ★

A hip clothes store in a side street just a short distance from Deák Ferenc Square. Over two floors, you can admire unique creations from young Hungarian designers alongside vintage pieces from all over the world. Plenty for men too. *Anker köz 2 | retrock.com | metro 1, 2, 3: Deák Ferenc tér | District VI | ⬚ d9*

25 SISKO STUDIO

This shop is only open on Thursdays (noon–7pm), but it's well worth a visit. It sells trendy and sustainable clothing and accessories from Hungarian designers, and nail artists can paint your nails with fun designs. They even do tattoos here! *Somogyi Béla utca 18 | studiosisko.com | metro 2 | tram 4, 6 Blaha Lujza tér | District VIII | ⬚ F10*

26 TIPTON EYEWORKS

Redesign for fans of vinyl. For Zachary Tipton, the Hungarian-American founder of Tipton Eyeworks, the story began in 1998 when he discovered his father's old record collection in the garage. He started making frames from them and the result is just plain cool – a must for glasses-wearing music lovers! *Showroom: Erkel utca 6 | tiptonbudapest.com | metro 4: Kálvin ter | District IX | ⬚ e11*

PORCELAIN, POTTERY & GLASS

27 AJKA KRISTÁLY

You think Bohemia crystal is special? Then check out the magnificent glass art originating from Ajka in the west of Hungary, which is easily on a par with the legendary crystal. The glassware is finely crafted and surprisingly understated in design. The store's antique interior design is also special, with its delightful wood carvings. Don't be put off by the unappealing exterior. *Kossuth Lajos utca 10 | FB: ajka crystal | metro 2: Astoria | tram 47, 48, 49 | District V | ⬚ d10*

28 HEREND PORCELAIN ★

You might think that porcelain is always kitsch and old-fashioned. You'd be wrong! Visit this shop selling porcelain by the legendary Herend. This vintage brand is world-famous and has managed to preserve its tradition for almost 200 years. Many of the contemporary designs are on a par with the porcelain craftsmanship of the past. *József Nádor tér 10–11 | herend.com | metro 1: Vörösmarty tér | District V | ⬚ d9 | Branch: Andrássy út 16 | metro 1: Opera | District VI | ⬚ D8*

29 ZSOLNAY

This porcelain manufacturer, based in the southern Hungarian city of Pécs, achieved fame for its colourful tiles that decorate many of Budapest's magnificent 19th-century Wilhelminian-style. The company is also synonymous with Art Nouveau in Hungary, and is known for its fine pieces. *József Nádor tér 12 | zsolnay budapest.com | metro 1, 2, 3: Deák Ferenc tér | District V | ⬚ d9*

SHOES

30 TISZA CIPŐ ★

This Communist-era brand has managed to achieve cult status. Young Hungarians are rediscovering these shoes with the stylized "T" as a cool alternative to conventional labels. The brand also includes women's and men's sportswear, bags and rucksacks. The name is taken from Hungary's second largest river, the Tisza. *Károly körút 1 | tiszacipo.hu | metro 2: Astoria | tram 47, 47B, 48, 49 | District VII | ▥ e10*

31 VASS

Vass is an institution! The hand-made shoes from this traditional workshop are equal to any made-to-measure items from London. The shop sells ready-to-wear shoes for men and women, or you can have your measurements taken for your very own made-to-measure pair. *Haris köz 6 | vass-shoes.com | metro 3: Ferenciek tere | District V | ▥ d10*

WINE & SPIRITS

32 BORTÁRSASÁG ★

Hungary makes excellent wines, from the sun-drenched grape-growing regions in the south of Villány, Pécs and Szekszárd, to the famous wine regions Tokaj and Eger in the north. The wine-trading company Bortársaság also operates its own, well-stocked wine shop. *Vécsey utca 5, corner of Vértanúk tere | bortarsasag.hu | metro 2: Kossuth Lajos tér | tram 2 | District V | ▥ C8*

33 PÁLINKA HOUSE

Hungarian fruit brandies *(pálinka)* have won several awards at top European spirits' fair Destillata, in Austria. Products from the top distilleries can be found here. *Rákóczi út 17 | magyarpalinkahaza.hu | metro 2: Astoria | tram 47, 48, 49 | District VIII | ▥ e10*

Elegant handmade shoes at Vass

NIGHTLIFE

You can party the night away in Budapest, whether on a party boat, rooftop terrace or in a "ruin pub". But away from the vibrant bars and clubbing scene, the city has even more to offer.

"Budapest by night" may sound like a phrase from a kitsch postcard, but the city does have its own kind of magical charm in the evenings, which attracts many locals to head to the pubs and clubs or to take a stroll after sunset. One thing's for sure: if you're not a party animal and loud nightlife isn't your scene, you should probably

You'll find all the venues in this chapter on the pull-out map 🗺

Spend a summer evening in the city's beer gardens

avoid the Jewish Quarter and Nagymezö utca, the street at the heart of the city's nightlife district. But luckily the city has plenty of alternative destinations to choose from.

A visit to the opera is a must for the fantastic ambience alone. Musicals have a firm place on the city's entertainment scene, and operetta has continued to assert itself successfully in the home of Franz Léhar and Imre Kálmán. Information on events, from techno parties to opera, can be found on *welovebudapest.com*.

WHERE TO GO OUT IN BUDAPEST

ÚJLIPÓTVÁROS

📍 Budapest Jazz Club ★

📍 Bambi Eszpresszó ★

Nyugati pályaudvar

Teréz körút

Vác út

Lehel utca

ARTHOUSE CINEMAS
Fantastic films just a few minutes' walk from each other

Carl Lutz rakpart

Szehlo Gábor rakpart

Duna (Donau)

Id. Antall József rakpart

Bajcsy-Zsilinszky út

Erzsébet körút

Művész ★

Toldi ★

Arany János utca Ⓜ

Liszt Ferenc
Academy of Music
(Zeneakadémia) ★

Opera House (Operaház) ★

Ⓜ Opera

Bajcsy-Zsilinszky út

VÁR

Attila út

BARS IN THE JEWISH QUARTER
The Quarter has earned its reputation as the Party District

LIPÓTVÁROS

Friedrich Born rakpart

Szimpla Kert ★

Astoria Ⓜ

Rákóczi út

Puskin ★

KRISZTINAVÁROS

BELVÁROS

ALL-NIGHT CLUBBING
Dance and party into the early morning

Hegyalja út

TABÁN

Gellérthegy

Üllői út

Duna (Donau)

Közraktár utca

Henryk Slawik rakpart

Karolina út

GELLÉRTHEGY

📍 A38 ★

Nagyszőlős utca

Bartók Béla út

Irinyi József utca

Petőfi híd

LÁGYMÁNYOS

Dürer Kert ★ 📍

HERMINAMEZŐ

Városliget

Dózsa György út

Andrássy út

TERÉZVÁROS

Thököly út

Kerepesi út

KEREPESDŰLŐ

Hintaló Iszoda ★

Fiumei út

József körút

Rákóczi tér

JÓZSEFVÁROS

DISTRICT VIII

What a thrill! The heart of Budapest's underground scene

KÖZÉPSŐ-FERENCVÁROS

Soroksári út

Palace of Arts
(Művészetek Palotája) ★

500 m
546 yd

MARCO POLO HIGHLIGHTS

★ **BAMBI ESZPRESSZÓ**
Travel back to Communist days over a coffee or fruit syrup ➤ p. 94

★ **HINTALÓ ISZODA**
Craft beer in a relaxed, cosy atmosphere ➤ p. 96

★ **SZIMPLA KERT**
There's always something happening in Budapest's first "ruin pub" ➤ p. 96

★ **MŰVÉSZ, PUSKIN, TOLDI**
Arthouse cinemas with that certain something ➤ p. 97

★ **LISZT FERENC ACADEMY OF MUSIC**
A harmony of architecture and music ➤ p. 99

★ **OPERA HOUSE**
Magnificent musical theatre ➤ p. 99

★ **PALACE OF ARTS**
Home to the top address for classical concerts – National Concert Hall Béla Bartók ➤ p. 100

★ **A38**
Rock and pop on a ship at anchor ➤ p. 100

★ **BUDAPEST JAZZ CLUB**
Talented international jazz musicians and a fine-dining menu ➤ p. 101

★ **DÜRER KERT**
Beer garden and concert venue in one ➤ p. 101

Yes, it's a little cheesy, but that doesn't stop it being true: music will always be a balm for the soul. Live music, especially, can have a wonderfully relaxing effect. And there is no shortage of musical talent in Hungary. We recommend the following: Veronika Harcsa *(harcsaveronika.hu)* studied jazz singing at the Academy of Music and has a wonderfully versatile voice. She is often on the road with her band *Bin-Jip*. Rozina Pátkai *(rozina patkai.com)*, meanwhile, has Italian roots and yet sings bossa nova in Portuguese on her album *Vocé e Eu –* a definite balm! For a different musical direction, try popular indie band *Szabó Benedek és a Galaxisok (szabobenedek.bandcamp.com)*. Their lyrics tackle the everyday problems that face Budapest millennials. All three reguarly give concerts in the capital, so why not try and make it to one of their gigs?

WHERE TO START?

An evening out in Budapest is best spent in the **Jewish Quarter** (🗺 *D–E9*), also known as the Party District *(bulinegyed)*. The more alternative hotspots around Madách Imre tér and in the Gozsdu Court offer something for everyone. Budapest is famous for its "ruin pubs" and the colourful *Szimpla Kert* is arguably the best choice. On warm summer evenings, city dwellers gather along the **Danube** – music fans love the concert ship *A38* on the Buda side.

BARS & PUBS

1 BAMBI ESZPRESSZÓ ★

A place where you can still experience the authentic *presszó* culture of the traditional neighbourhood pub/bar. With its red leather furniture, white lace tablecloths and yellow retro mosaics, time seems to have stood still in Bambi since it opened in the 1960s, and yet this popular spot has retained its charm. Even the menu throws up old Hungarian classics such as *melegszendvics* (a slice of white bread with melted cheese and ketchup), debrecener sausages, cakes, coffee, beer and fruit syrups. You can sit outside or inside among the old men playing traditional board games. *Mon–Fri 7am–10pm, Sat/Sun 9am–10pm | Frankel Leó utca 2–4 | FB: bambi eszpresszo | tram 4, 6 Margit híd, budai hídfő | District II | 🗺 B7*

2 CSENDES LÉTTEREM

The Csendes chain has spread across Budapest, with not just one but three attractive locations. The Létterem venue was the first of its kind – a relaxed, creatively decorated mix of bar, café and restaurant, whose main clientele are students from the nearby ELTE university. The wine and snack bar *Csendes Társ* and the *Csendes Concept Store* are all just a stone's throw away near Károlyi Kert. *Tue–Sat 6pm–midnight | Ferenczy István utca 7 | FB: csendesvinatagebar | metro 2: Astoria | tram 47, 47B, 48, 49 | District V | 🗺 e10*

Nostalgia with your ketchup: back to the sixties at Bambi Eszpresszó

3 ÉLESZTŐHÁZ

You can order any drink you like… As long as it's beer! Those who can't get enough of the malt beverage will feel at home here, sitting either in the courtyard or the spacious interior decorated with bare red-brick walls and contemporary wooden furniture. They serve mainly Hungarian craft beers and ales – try, for example, the tasty mint chocolate stout brewed by the Szent András brewery. *The Vino-Piano Wine & Tapas Bar* next door makes sure you don't starve after your copious beer consumption. *Sun/Mon 3pm–1am, Tue/Wed 3pm–2am, Thur–Sat 3pm–3am | Tűzoltó utca 22 | elesztohaz.hu | metro 3: Corvin-negyed | tram 3, 4 | District IX | ⌨ F11*

4 HÁROM HOLLÓ/THREE RAVENS

Opened by German writer, translator and university lecturer Wilhelm Droste, this coffee house harks back to the Budapest coffee house culture of the 1900s. It opened its doors on 22 November 2017, and the date is no coincidence: it would have been the 140th birthday of the great Hungarian poet Endre Ady – and his favourite coffee house was called what? Yup, you've got it: Három Holló! But what you don't see right away

INSIDER TIP
Hidden cultural centre

from the outside is that Három Holló is not just a coffee house but also a buzzing cultural centre, filling a real gap in the Budapest arts scene.

Venture inside and you'll find a live concert one day; the next day there could be a theatre performance or exhibition. As a nice extra, the audience is always a good mix of ages. A reasonable lunch menu is served from Monday to Friday. *Daily noon–midnight | Piarista köz 1 (entrance from Szabadsajtó út) | haromhollo.hu/de | tram 2: Március 15. tér | metro 3: Ferenciek tere | District V | ⌑ d10*

5 HINTALÓ ISZODA ★

There's an old Hungarian proverb that says: "A wise man deserves a good horse." You'll certainly find that here at the Hintaló (Rocking Horse)! This bar is cosy, artistic and playful – and hard to leave after the last beer. Speaking of beer, it somehow tastes extra good here, with six local varieties on tap and dozens of other bottled craft beers. Plus, there are often live concerts – and, with a bit of luck, barman Omar will treat you to a mezcal. *Daily 6pm–midnight | Bacsó Béla utca 15 | FB: hintalobudapest | tram 4, 6 | metro 2: Blaha Lujza tér | District VIII | ⌑ F10*

6 KISÜZEM

Large windows, bricks, plants and bird cages: Kisüzem is a pub that falls somewhere between cosy and artistic. The walls are usually adorned with works by Hungarian artists, from risograph prints featuring political satire to abstract paintings. Good, if concise, menu. *Daily | Kis Diófa utca 2 | to book tel. 1 7 81 67 05 (except Fri/Sat from 8pm) | FB: Kisuzem | tram 4, 6 Király utca/Erzsébet körút | metro 2: Blaha Lujza tér | District VII | ⌑ e9*

7 MARXIM PUB

To find the entrance to this pub, just follow the red star – the symbol of socialism. On entering the world of Marxim, you'll find yourself surrounded by a bust of Lenin, a wire fence and other Soviet-style props. On the menu is delicious pizza with homemade tomato sauce and a small selection of craft beers from the Szent András brewery. Don't forget to check out the fresco on the wall in the back room… *Daily | Kis Rókus utca 23 | FB: marxim pub | tram 4, 6: Mechwart liget | District II | ⌑ A7*

8 MIKA TIVADAR KERT

"Kert" means garden, and this large, atmospheric beer garden is a great place to enjoy the warmer months. The clientele is mostly young Hungarian students and international visitors. Only open in summer. *Mon/Tue 4pm–midnight, Wed 4pm–1am, Thur 4pm–2am, Fri/Sat 4pm–3am | Kazinczy utca 47 | FB: mikativadar mulato | metro 1: Opera | District VII | ⌑ e9*

9 SZIMPLA KERT ★ ⚑

Szimpla Kert was the first of Budapest's extremely hyped "ruin pubs", and it attracts crowds of tourists and expats. Surrounded by crumbling walls, the courtyard garden is particularly popular in summer, when you can smoke shishas. It's worth taking a peek at all the wildly decorated rooms inside. Surprisingly, this legendary ruin bar is actually most fun in the afternoon, when

INSIDER TIP
Afternoon delight

NIGHTLIFE

you can enjoy a simple homemade lemonade in peace, in an atmosphere far from the hustle and bustle of the nightlife scene. *Daily from noon | Kazinczy utca 14 | szimpla.hu | metro 2: Astoria | tram 47, 48, 49 | District VII | ⌑ e9*

🔟 TELEP

What started life as a small pub for skateboarders and the hip-hop scene has become an extremely popular hangout for trendy young city dwellers. On the first floor is a small, hip shop that sometimes hosts exhibitions. The typical Telep visitor is a full-bearded, tattooed man with a dog, who sips on a Club-Mate. The *Központ* diagonally opposite belongs to the same proprietor and is similar in style. In summer, both venues host the party outside – mainly because most of the clientele are smokers! *Mon–Wed noon–midnight, Thur–Sat noon–2am, Sun noon–10pm | Madách Imre út 8 | FB: TelepGaleria | metro 1, 2, 3: Deák Ferenc tér | tram 47, 48, 49 | District VII | ⌑ e9*

🔟🔟 360 BAR

A fantastic rooftop bar. The origin of the name is quite simple: the roof offers a 360-degree panoramic view of Pest – a privilege you pay for with your food and drink! Hot tip: you can still visit the bar in winter without freezing thanks to the transparent, heated igloos upstairs. Perfect for fondue or mulled wine! It's a good idea to book (can be done online). *Mon–Thur 5pm–midnight, Fri/Sat 2pm–2am, Sun2pm–midnight | Fri–*

Pop in to Kisüzem for drinks and art

Sun 1000 Ft. admission | Andrássy út 39 | 360bar.hu | metro 1: Oktogon | tram 2, 4 | District VI | ⌑ E8

CINEMAS

🔟🔟 ARTHOUSE CINEMAS

Budapest has lots going for it when it comes to arthouse cinemas. These are three of the cosiest, showing films from all over the world with Hungarian subtitles, while Hungarian films usually are shown with English subtitles. The *Művész*, in particular, is well worth a visit and offers five screens. The *Toldi*, meanwhile, is a good spot to party the night away after the film, as it hosts regular club nights and concerts.

INSIDER TIP
Party at the cinema

97

artmozi.hu | ★ *Művész: Teréz körút 30 | metro 3: Nyugati pályauvar | District VI |* ⊞ *E8* | ★ *Puskin: Kossuth Lajos utca 18 | metro 3: Ferenciek tere | District V |* ⊞ *e10* | ★ *Toldi: Bajcsy-Zsilinszky út 36–38 | metro 3: Arany János utca | District V |* ⊞ *D8*

🔢 URÁNIA

Believe it or not, the Uránia cinema has been showing (documentary) films for over 100 years – today it is also a venue for concerts, ballet performances, public readings and also hosts a coffee shop. The building is a stunning piece of architecture, both inside and out, combining Venetian Gothic, Italian Renaissance and Arabic-Moorish styles. In other words: don't miss it! *Rákóczi út 25 | urania-nf.hu | metro 2: Blaha Lujza tér | bus 7 | District VII |* ⊞ *e10*

CONCERTS, OPERA & OPERETTA

🔢 BUDAPEST MUSIC CENTER

The BMC is a dream come true for trombonist and music instructor László Gőz, who founded the cultural and information centre with music database and library in 1996. Featuring a neoclassical façade and contemporary interior, the building is an excellent piece of architecture. Sophisticated chamber music and high-quality jazz are played in the ✈ *Opus Jazz Club (admission approx. 8–15 euros)* and the concert hall is a popular venue for pop and classical music.

INSIDER TIP Dinner with jazz

The restaurant here will knock your socks off in terms of both variety and quality. And there's a lunch

Enjoy live jazz, pop or classical at the Budapest Music Center

menu, too. *Mon–Sat 9am–10pm | Mátyás utca 8 | Tel. 1 216 7894 | bmc. hu | metro 3, 4: Kálvin tér | tram 47, 47B, 48, 49 | District IX | 🚇 e11*

🔢 LISZT FERENC ACADEMY OF MUSIC (ZENEAKADÉMIA) ⭐

A masterpiece both inside and out – the Franz Liszt Academy of Music is Hungary's most influential music school, with an excellent international reputation. It's a great place to hear classical music played by academy students. The building's façade (completed in 1907 and extensively renovated in 2013) is striking, and the foyer and large hall are splendid examples of Hungarian Art Nouveau. There is no need to pre-book; tickets are available at the box office. *No performances July/Aug | regular 50-minute guided tours in English (4,700 Ft.) | Liszt Ferenc tér 8 | tel. 1 462 4600 | lisztacademy.hu | metro 1: Oktogon | tram 4, 6 Király utca | District VI | 🚇 E8*

🔢 COMEDY THEATRE (VÍGSZÍNHÁZ)

The theatre, opened in 1896, is a masterpiece of architectural eclecticism, even from the outside. Performances include classics such as Shakespeare and Friedrich Dürrenmatt. There are also other good productions you can enjoy without understanding Hungarian, such as *The Jungle Book* or *The Wizard of Oz*. *No performances June–Sept | Szent István körút 14 | tel. 1 329 3920 | vigszinhaz.hu/english | tram 2, 4, 6 Jászai Mari tér | District XIII | 🚇 D7*

🔢 OPERA HOUSE (OPERAHÁZ) ⭐

The Opera House is renowned for staging great works from Italian opera and international ballet to Hungarian classical music. Accompanying the programme is the visual pleasure of the surroundings. During an interval, standing on one of the balconies that look out on Andrássy út is a special experience. The Opera was closed for a number of years for renovations, but it reopened in 2022 and is as stunning as ever. Sadly, the quality of the actual performances has declined somewhat and the staging tends towards the kitsch. Still, you can often grab a seat at the top of the gallery – albeit with a poorer view – for just 1,500 Ft. Tickets are available online or from the opera shop (daily 10am–7pm). *Andrássy út 22 | opera.hu | metro 1: Opera | District VI | 🚇 D–E8*

🔢 OPERETTA THEATRE (OPERETT-SZÍNHÁZ)

Operetta may seem slightly old-fashioned, but this music theatre, situated on the "Budapest Broadway", puts on contemporary and intellectually demanding pieces. Its repertoire includes *The Gypsy Princess* by Hungarian composer Emmerich Kálmán, *The Hunchback of Notre-Dame* and *Romeo and Juliet*. The ideal place to see a performance is in the freshly renovated *Kálmán Imre Teátrum* auditorium. *Nagymező utca 17 | tel. 1 312 4866 | operett.hu | metro 1: Opera | District VI | 🚇 E8*

All aboard the A38 – club, restaurant and music venue on the Danube

🗓 PALACE OF ARTS (MŰVÉSZETEK PALOTÁJA) ★

What a sound! The National Béla Bartók Concert Hall, with its 1,700 seats, is the core of the Palace of Arts (MüPa for short). Its acoustics are a marvel of modern engineering, while the design, featuring light-coloured wood, is also something to behold. This concert hall sees performances by the Hungarian National Philharmonic Orchestra as well as major orchestras and soloists from around the world. Modern musicians, too, such as Joanna Newsom and Mark Kozelek have also trod the boards here. *Komor Marcell utca 1 | mupa.hu/en | tram 2, 24 Müpa-Nemzeti Színház | District IX | ⌘ F14*

MUSIC VENUES & CLUBS

🗓 A38 ★

OK, it might be a little unusual, but moored on the Buda side, the A38 is a decommissioned Ukrainian stone hauler that is now the city's most popular live-music venue. There is a great restaurant on the upper deck while the ship's hull provides fantastic acoustics for live concerts. In terms of genre, expect rock, metal and punk as well as pop, rap and electronic. *Random Trip* is a series of concerts where young talented musicians

INSIDER TIP
Hungary's young talent

from the Hungarian music scene perform. *Daily | restaurant Mon–Fri 10am–10pm, Sat 4pm–10pm | Buda side of the Petőfi bridge | a38.hu/en | tram 4, 6: Petőfi híd, Budai hídfő | District XI | ⌘ E13*

21 AETHER CLUB

Once a mere basement club on the periphery of Gozsdu Court, this venue has become so legendary among the city's techno fans that it now even sells its own merchandise. Regular international DJs ensure you can dance the night away here with confidence. *Fri, Sat 11pm–6am | Király utca 13 | aether club.com | metro 1, 2, 3: Deák Ferenc tér | tram 47, 48, 49 | District VII | ▥ e9*

22 AKVÁRIUM

When the sun shines through the man-made pool that covers this semi-outdoor venue, it becomes apparent how it got its name – the interior of the Akvárium (aquarium) is flooded by what look like blue waves. During the day it's a relaxed café, bar and restaurant, and in the evenings DJs play live. The central venue also hosts the odd '90s or Halloween-themed party. *Daily from 3pm | Erzsébet tér | akvariumklub.hu/en | metro 1, 2, 3: Deák Ferenc tér | tram 47, 48, 49 | District V | ▥ d9*

23 ALTEREGO

Budapest's most popular gay club is open to everyone and attracts a diverse crowd. A special highlight are the trans variety shows at midnight. Friday is karaoke night, held in the smaller of the club's two rooms. *Fri 10pm–5am, Sat 10pm–6am | Dessewffy utca 33 | alteregoclub.hu | tram 4, 6 Oktogon | District VI | ▥ D8*

 INSIDER TIP **Trans-tastic!**

24 AURÓRA & GÓLYA

These two independent, progressive cultural centres both offer great programmes of events, ranging from concerts and record fairs to exhibitions and board game parties. They are also home to civil organisations and artists. If you feel more at home in alternative circles and the underground scene, they will quickly win you over. Unfortunately the city government has been threatening to close them for years, so make sure to visit soon. *Auróra: Auróra utca 11 | FB: aurora unofficial | tram 4, 6 Rákóczi tér | metro 4: II János Pál pápa tér | District VIII | ▥ F10 | Gólya: Orczy út 46-48 | FB: golyaszovetkezet | metro 3: Klinikák | District VIII | ▥ H11*

25 BUDAPEST JAZZ CLUB ★

Budapest's number one location for jazz warmly welcomes both newcomers and aficionados to its casual venue. Located in the pretty district of Újlipótváros, the club hosts both Hungarian and international jazz musicians. You can order drinks and light snacks from the tables in front of the stage, while those with a larger appetite should visit the extremely tempting bistro. *Tue 10.30am–midnight, Wed/Thur 10.30am–1am, Fri 10.30am–2am, Sat 4pm–2am, Sun opening hours vary | Hollán Ernő utca 7 | table and ticket reservations: tel. 1 798 7289 | bjc.hu/home | tram 2, 4, 6: Jászai Mari tér | District XIII | ▥ D6*

26 DÜRER KERT ★

The Dürer is a real institution among Hungarians who like alternative rock…

and a quick game of table tennis in the beer garden, or a good comic festival. Originally, this venue was located near the municipal forest, before its controversial eviction at the hands of the construction companies. Still, the power of hindsight suggests this was no bad thing: its new location right next to the Danube is somehow even better. The Dürer welcomes dogs and has a play park for children. It also dishes up tasty burgers and has bicycle racks! *Öböl utca 1 | durerkert.com/en | tram 1: Hengermalom út/Szerémi út | bus 33E, 33 Hengermalom út | District XI | ▥ D15*

²⁷ INSTANT FOGAS

Located in an old city townhouse in Pest, this crazy party complex is not just a run-of-the-mill ruin pub, but offers a garden, an entertainment centre with dart boards, table football and so on. There's a techno club on the first floor, while the *Robot* punk and rock club is in the basement. Also on the premises are the *Liebling* restaurant and several dancefloors playing a wide spectrum of music. The venue often hosts concerts or DJs from abroad and attracts an international, party-loving crowd. The late opening hours speak for themselves! *Daily 5pm–6am | Akácfa utca 49–51 | instant-fogas.com | tram 4, 6: Király utca | District VII | ▥ E9*

²⁸ KLUB VITTULA

Yes, the entrance is a little dubious looking, the dark stairs even more so, but we promise you're in for some wonderfully chaotic underground fun

here. Whether it's for an acid house party or a raw punk concert, or even if you just drop in for a quick beer at the bar, a visit to the Vittula never fails to be an authentic experience. *Mon 6pm–midnight, Tue–Sat 6pm–2am | Kertész utca 4 | FB: klubvittula | tram 4, 6: Wesselényi utca/Erzsébet körút | District VII | ▥ F9*

DANCE & FOLK MUSIC

²⁹ FONÓ (FONÓ BUDAI ZENEHÁZ)

The Fonó Music House in Buda has a comprehensive, colourful culture and entertainment programme, spanning folk and world music. The venue also hosts a regular *táncház* (dance house) with a great atmosphere – check the website for dates. Join in and don't be shy; the dance instructors will show you the necessary moves. A spin

Experimental modern dance is staged at Tráfó

around the dancefloor is to experience for yourself what the flirtation between tradition and passion feels like in Hungary. *Mon–Wed 10am–9pm, Thur 10am–11pm, Fri 10am–2am, Sat 2–11pm | Sztregova utca 3 | fono.hu | tram 17, 41, 47, 48, 56, 61: Kalotaszeg utca | District IX | ⃞ C15*

⒁ NATIONAL DANCE THEATRE (NEMZETI TANCSZÍNHÁZ)

After some back and forth, all because the prime minister, Viktor Orbán, was determined to have his office at the National Dance Theatre's previous home in the Buda Palace Theatre, a solution was finally been found. The National Dance Theatre, founded in 2001, has been based in the *Millenáris* cultural and leisure centre for some time now. The repertoire is varied – sometimes classical, sometimes modern, sometimes Hungarian, sometimes Indian. Discover the latest repertoire and performances on the website. *Kis Rókus utca 16–20 | nemzetitancszinhaz.hu | tram 4, 6, 17, 19: Széna tér | District II | ⃞ A7*

⒂ TRÁFÓ

You'll find all sorts of different things at Trafó, from film screenings and small exhibitions to concerts and theatre. But the real treat here is contemporary dance: lose yourself in experimental and innovative performances from both Hungarian and international artists. We strongly recommend local companies like *Frenák Pál* and *Duda Éva Társulat*. *Liliom utca 41 | trafo.hu/en | tram 4, 6: Corvin-negyed | District IX | ⃞ F11*

ACTIVE & RELAXED

The city and the beach come together in perfect harmony at The Beachclub

SPORT & WELLNESS

BEER IN A SPA

Beer and spa in one? Yes you heard correctly; the 🍴 *Beer Spa (daily 11am–7pm | admission 17,000 Ft., combination ticket with the Széchenyi Baths 25, 350 Ft. | Állatkerti körút 9–11 | tel. 30 515 0702 | thermalbeerspa. com | metro 1: Széchenyi fürdő | District XIV | 🚇 G6)* offers guests the chance to relax in wooden tubs filled with water heated to 36°C, with the addition of a mixture of malt, hops and yeast. Rich in Vitamin B, this blend is supposed to do wonders for your skin. You can, of course, also enjoy a beer and some Hungarian snacks while you bathe. 👥 Non-alcoholic drinks are also available, making the Beer Spa a family-friendly, fun experience.

CANOEING

Hungarians have a long history of success in all kinds of water sports. In fact, both the men's and women's teams won the most medals among countries at the 2018 World Canoe Championships. If you fancy trying your hand at canoeing, your best bet is to head down to the *Római-part* (Roman Beach) in the north of Budapest (District III). At the *Béke boathouse (Római Part 53 | beke csonakhaz.hu)*, you can hire a canoe for 4,500 Ft. and explore places like the Lupa-sziget islet.

ESCAPE GAMES

Let me out of here! The concept of escape rooms was invented in Hungary's capital, which is why the rooms here are real crowd-pullers. The original Budapest venues are also far more inventive and creative than the copy-cat rooms abroad. *E-Exit (Nyár utca 27 | szabadulos-jatek.hu)* has a number of rooms, including an exciting George Orwell-inspired *1984*

The glamorous Gellért Baths

escape room. The six tricky rooms at *Locked Room (Székely Mihály utca 4 | locked.hu)* are largely themed around films and TV series like *Breaking Bad* and *Zodiac*. You can also play here with just two of you.

FOOTBALL

"Morality, strength, consensus" is the motto of the *Fradi (FTC/Ferencvárosi Torna Club | fradi.hu/en)* football club, whose home stadium is the *Groupama Aréna (groupamaarena.com)*. The club dates back to 1899. Its big rival is *Újpest (Újpest Football Club | ujpestfc. hu)*, with its signature white and purple colours, based in the Szusza Ferenc stadium. Tickets for games at the latter are easy to buy online, while Fradi games require an overly complicated registration process on site. But no matter which team you are rooting for, the stadium atmosphere is well worth a visit.

JOGGING

On your marks, get set, go – *Margaret Island* (see p. 38) is the most popular spot in the city for jogging. The 5.5km trail, paved in rubber matting, loops around the island and offers scenic views of the Danube. There are no cars to disturb your run. Underneath the Margaret Bridge there's a 🐷 free outdoor *fitness studio*, with power training equipment to complete your fitness routine after your run.

THE WONDERS OF SCIENCE 👾

A 5,000m² space bursting with interactive scientific wonders: this is the *Csodák Palotája* or *Palace of Wonders (daily 10am–7pm | admission 4,400 Ft., children 3,200 Ft. | Bécsi út 38–44 | csopa.hu/en | tram 17, 19, 41: Kolosy tér | District II | 🗺 B4)*, or "CsoPa" for short. With more than 250 fun and educational games, it won't just be the kids who are amazed.

FESTIVALS & EVENTS

JANUARY
New Year's Day concerts are traditionally held in St Stephen's Basilica, featuring its majestic-sounding organ. Church music concerts take place on 2 January. *organconcert.hu/en*

APRIL
⭐ **Budapest Spring Festival:** A multi-week cultural festival with events and concerts from classical to jazz and folk, involving elite national artists as well as international stars. *btf.hu*

MAY
🐃 **Budapest 100:** Originally, the focus here was on the city's 100-year-old buildings. Now, it has grown into a series of events with open houses, guided tours, lectures and even a group breakfast. All free! *budapest100.hu/en*
International Comic Festival: Calling all fans of comics, manga and graphic novels! The festival is organised at *Dürer Kert (see p. 101)* in mid-May. *FB: kepregenyfesztival*

JUNE
Jewish Art Days Festival: Programme series in early June for anyone with an interest in Jewish culture. Concerts, parties, talks and theatre … Keep an eye out for performances by the *Budapest Klezmer Band* and *Budapest Bár. zsidomuveszetinapok.hu*
Night of Museums: Simply purchase a wristband (2,200 Ft.) to unlock access to dozens of Budapest museums (mid/late June). *muzej.hu/en*

JULY
Budapest Pride: Budapest residents have been out on the streets demonstrating for LGBTQ+ rights for over 20 years. Today, *Pride* is an enormous celebration for everyone who supports tolerance and an open-minded culture. *budapestpride.com*

The Sziget Festival is a huge party with music on all fronts

AUGUST

Sziget Festival: Held on Óbuda island (early/mid Aug), this diverse music festival is worth going to at least once in your lifetime (photo).

Formula 1 – Hungarian Grand Prix: The stars of international motorsports gather at the Hungaroring near Budapest. If you fancy a go at the wheel, try the go-kart track in the centre of the ring! *hungaroring.hu*

⭐ **St Stephen's Day:** On 20 August, to mark the national holiday commemorating Hungary's first king, Budapest holds a fireworks display on the Danube – with lots of *pálinka* (fruit brandy).

SEPTEMBER

Budapest Beer Week: International craft beer festival with high-quality produce from all around the globe, lectures from beer experts and delicious food (early/mid Sept). *bpbw.hu*

Spar Budapest Marathon: Autumn in Budapest is a time for marathons. A half marathon is also held in September. *runinbudapest.com*

NOVEMBER

Verzio International Human Rights Documentary Film Festival: The documentaries shown here are united by their attempts to deal with the ills of the world (mid Nov). *verzio.org/en*

DECEMBER

Christmas market: Vörösmarty tér fills with – admittedly somewhat overpriced – offerings like handicrafts, mulled wine and *kürtőskalács* (spit cake) as well as beautiful Christmas lights, especially on Andrássy út.

New Year's Eve: At least half of Budapest turns out to see in the new year. Several places have stages offering free live music, but the crowd also provides its own accompaniment on loud toy trumpets.

SLEEP WELL

THE ART OF SLEEPING...

... is taken literally at the boutique hotel *Brody House (10 rooms | Bródy Sándor utca 10 | tel. 1 323 7583 | brody.house | metro 3: Kálvin tér | €€ | District VIII | ▥ E10)*: the rooms are all individually furnished, some of them in an extremely extravagant design. Breakfast is served in the salon, which also contains a casual bar. Dating from 1896, the building has always been home to artists. Artist residencies are today held in the associated *Brody Studios (Vörösmarty utca 38 | District VI | ▥ E7)*, which also has its own private club. Ask nicely and they might let you in!

BED DOWN WITH SOCIALISM

In the mood for a bit of retro? Then you'll love this tall, round tower: the *Hotel Budapest (280 rooms | Szilágyi Erzsébet fasor 47 | tel. 30 313 4005 | hotel-budapest.hu/en hotel-budapest. hu/en | tram 17, 19, 41, 56, 59, 61: Városmajor | bus 5, 22, 91, 105, 155, 156, 222 | € | District II | ▥ 0)*. The 15-storey "round hotel" (*körszálló*, as the locals call it) on the Buda side opened back in 1967 and has retained its Socialist-era charm to this day. Perfect if you love 1960s design, and value peace, quiet and closeness to nature. The Széll Kálmán tér transport hub is just a few minutes away.

ART NOUVEAU TO DREAM OF

No exaggeration, the *Four Seasons Gresham Palace (169 rooms | Széchenyi István tér 5–6 | tel. 1 268 6000 | fourseasons.com/budapest | metro 1: Vörösmarty tér | tram 2: Széchenyi István tér | €€€ | District V | ▥ C9)* is Budapest's most stunning hotel. No surprise, then, that rock and Hollywood stars have spent the night here (including the Red Hot Chili Peppers and Anthony Hopkins).

Sweet dreams at Brody House are followed by breakfast in the salon

You can take a peek inside by treating yourself to the *Herend Afternoon Tea (daily 3–6pm)*.

AT ONE WITH NATURE

Explore the Buda Hills without losing touch with the city – there's no better starting point than *Ave Natura Camping (Csermely utca | tel. 70 550 7069 | campingavenatura.hu | bus 291 Zugliget | District XII | ⌘ 0)*, a small, cosy campsite. Rustic, yes, but always clean. You can easily set off on a hike from here, and the *Zugligeti Libegő* chairlift, taking you up a wooded hill, is just a few minutes away on foot. The air remains pleasant, even in summer.

ESTABLISHMENT WITH VINTAGE CHARM

Painter and designer Ádám Szarvas and his team have created a feel-good hostel for individualistic dreamers in the *Lavender Circus Hostel (15 twin rooms | Múzeum körút 37 | tel. 70 417 7763 | lavendercircus.com | metro 3, 4: Kálvin tér | tram 47, 48, 49 | € | District V | ⌘ E10*. Decorated with great attention to detail, it feels like a cosy flat shared by artists. This centrally located, yet quiet, spot is very family friendly – there is space in each room for a cot.

A BED ON THE DANUBE

You'll find a "waterbed" of a different kind at *Vogue (2 rooms | Carl Lutz rakpart 1 | tel. 30 942 5027 | restaurantvogue.hu | tram 2, 4, 6: Jászai Mari tér | € | District XIII | ⌘ D5)*. It's a ship that has been anchored here for 20 years with two rooms for guests. It functions mainly as a restaurant – the kind of place people go to for dinner on special occasions. The wood-rich interior creates a cosy atmosphere, but the selling points are the price, location and the view (of the Danube and Margaret Island).

DISCOVERY
TOURS

Do you want to get under the skin of the city? Then these discovery tours provide the perfect guide. They include advice on which sights to visit, tips on where to stop for that perfect holiday snap, a choice of the best places to eat and drink and suggestions for fun activities.

The view from the Fisherman's Bastion will take your breath away

DISCOVERY TOURS OVERVIEW

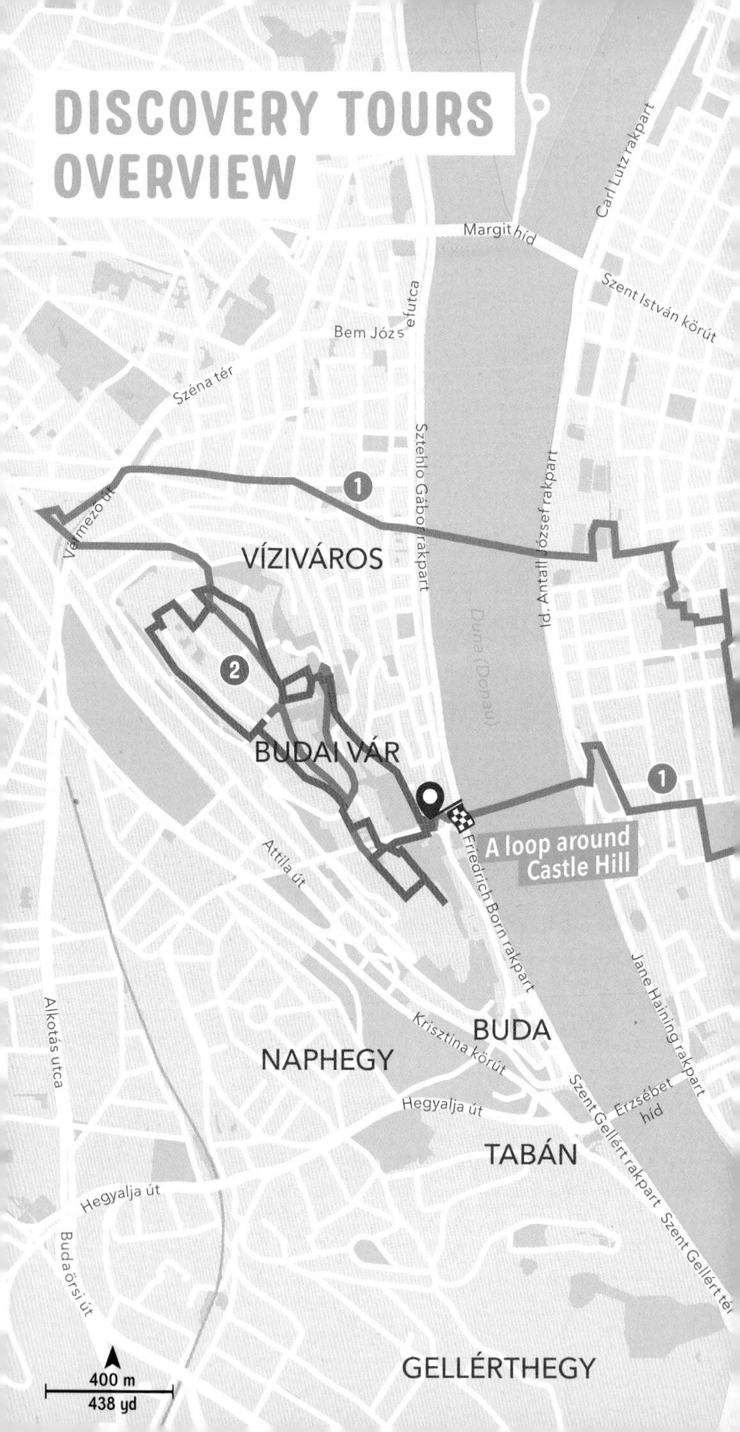

Margit híd

Carl Lutz rakpart

Szent István körút

Bem Józs e f utca

Széna tér

Szehlo Gábor rakpart

①

VÍZIVÁROS

Vámező út

Id. Antall József rakpart

Duna (Donau)

②

BUDAI VÁR

①

Friedrich Born rakpart

📍🏁 **A loop around Castle Hill**

Attila út

Jane Haining rakpart

Alkotás utca

Krisztina körút

BUDA

NAPHEGY

Hegyalja út

Szent Gellért rakpart

Erzsébet híd

TABÁN

Hegyalja út

Szent Gellért tér

Budaörsi út

GELLÉRTHEGY

400 m
438 yd

ÚJLIPÓTVÁROS

Váci út

Léhel utca

Váci út

Teréz körút

TERÉZVÁROS

Andrássy út

Erzsébet körút

1

Dózsa György út

Városliget

ERZSÉBETVÁROS

Thököly út

Baross tér

3

Elizabeth Town: a tour of the old Jewish Quarter

Fiumei út

Rákóczi út

Károly körút

Rákóczi út

Budapest at a glance

Kálvin tér

PALOTANEGYED

József körút

JÓZSEFVÁROS

Szent Gellért tér

Üllői út

CORVIN NEGYED

Közraktár utca

Ferenc körút

Üllői út

❶ BUDAPEST AT A GLANCE

➤ The Castle District in the morning, a ruin pub in the evening
➤ See both Buda and Pest at their best
➤ Stop off at the thermal baths

📍	Deák Ferenc tér	🏁	Deák Ferenc tér
🔄	18km	🚶	1 day, 3 hrs total walking/ travel time

Costs: public transport 1,650 Ft. (24-hour ticket with a Budapest Card)

ℹ️ **Matthias Church** is often closed on Saturday afternoons for weddings. No visitors allowed on Sunday mornings during church services
Remember to pack: swimwear

❶ Deák Ferenc tér

❷ Széchenyi Chain Bridge

❸ Castle Hill

START THE DAY WITH A VIEW

Start your day in Budapest with a trip to the Castle District in Buda. The best place to start your tour is the central traffic junction ❶ Deák Ferenc tér at the centre of the Pest side of the city. *From there, take bus 16 over the* ❷ Széchenyi Chain Bridge ➤ p. 41 *to the Buda side of the city.* From the funicular station *(Sikló)*, the bus makes its ascent up ❸ Castle Hill, where you get off at the Dísz tér bus stop. On your left is the impressive Buda Castle ➤ p. 34. *If you follow Tárnok utca on your right to Szentháromság tér,* you'll come across two city highlights.

The majestic Matthias church ➤ p. 36 stands *on Szentháromság tér*, with the playful and romantic Fisherman's Bastion ➤ p. 36 in front, providing wonderful views over the city. Take a short coffee break *on Szentháromság utca* at the famous Biedermeier-style café Ruszwurm Cukrászda *(daily | Szentháromság utca 7 | ruszwurm.hu),* before enjoying a relaxing stroll *along Hess András tér and Fortuna utca to Bécsi kapu tér.*

AN ARCHITECTURAL MIX AND A BASILICA

Take the bus (16, 16A, 116) from Bécsi kapu tér to Széll Kálmán tér and from there the metro line 2 to Kossuth Lajos tér by the ❹ Parliament Building ➤ p. 39. A walk through the streets of Leopold Town *(Lipótváros)* will sum up the meaning of the term "eclecticism" beautifully: the different architectural styles come together to produce a visual treat. *Head along Báthory utca and turn right on Honvéd utca,* where house no. 3 is the ❺ House of Hungarian Art Nouveau (Magyar szecesszió háza) *(closed Sun | magyarszecessziohaza. hu),* with its splendid Art Nouveau façade and authentic Art Nouveau café for an energising coffee break.

A few feet away is the park-like ❻ Szabadság tér ➤ p. 40 with splendid buildings dating back to the period of rapid industrial expansion in Europe. *Walk past the US embassy and take a left along Hold utca,* where you will be confronted by a masterpiece designed by the architect Ödön Lechner: the former ❼ Post Office Savings Bank *(Magyar Király Takarék*

❹ Parliament Building

❺ House of Hungarian Art Nouveau

❻ Szabadság tér

❼ Post Office Savings Bank

Take a welcome coffee break at Ruszwurm on Castle Hill

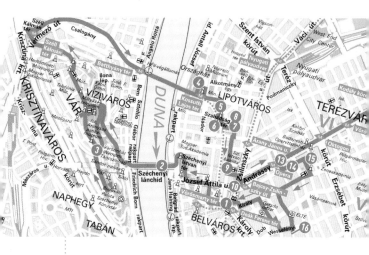

8 Indoor market hall	

Pénztár), which is today part of the National Bank. Directly opposite is the nice **8** indoor market hall, where you can stock up on your supplies with food from Hungarian small businesses. *Head south following Hercegprímás utca to* **9** St Stephen's Basilica ➤ p.41. Stop for a moment on Szent István tér: the outside of this neoclassical basilica, with its enormous dome, is almost as beautiful as the church's interior. Stop for lunch at one of the many cafés in the area.

9 St Stephen's Basilica

HEROES, ART AND AN AMUSEMENT PARK – THEN RELAX IN THE MAGNIFICENT BATHS

10 Andrássy út ➤ p.44 *starts behind the basilica on the left and the underground station Bajcsy-Zsilinszky út is situated there.* The historic *underground line 1 (Földalatti)* is an ideal way to explore this exclusive avenue. On **11** Heroes' Square ➤ p.46 (Hősök tere stop), where you will also find the Millennium Memorial, you will be right in the midst of Hungarian history. There is also some great art here at the Museum of Fine Arts ➤ p.47, which has its own café.

10 Andrássy út

11 Heroes' Square

From Heroes' Square, it's just a few feet to the **12** Municipal forest ➤ p.48, with its many attractions such as the romantic Vajdahunyad Castle ➤ p.50 or the Budapest Zoo ➤ p.49. Feeling tired? Then relax

12 Municipal forest

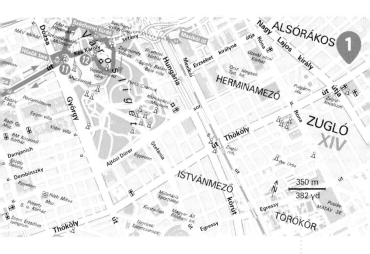

your mind and body in the palatial Széchenyi Baths ➤ p. 49 *(follow the signposts)*.

STUNNING OPERA FOLLOWED BY SOMETHING SWEET

Take the metro line 1 back to the Opera at Andrássy út. The magnificent ⑬ Opera House ➤ pp. 44 and 99 is surrounded by shops and restaurants, characterised by exquisite architecture. Time for a refreshment? Uniquely designed, crazy sweet treats, ice cream and coffee, as well as quirky bric-a-brac are available nearby at ⑭ 🍭 Sugar! *(daily | Paulay Ede utca 48 | sugarshop. hu)*. It's worthwhile having a look inside if you like bright colours!

INSIDER TIP
Sweet treats!

⑬ Opera House

⑭ Sugar!

A COSY SQUARE AND THE NIGHTLIFE DISTRICT

A few feet away is ⑮ Liszt Ferenc tér ➤ p. 44, with a wide selection of cafés, including Menza ➤ p. 74. Liszt Ferenc tér is also the ideal starting point for a stroll around the former Jewish Quarter. *Go along Király utca and then take a left into Kazinczy and enjoy a refreshment at one of its many cafés*, such as alternative bar ⑯ Szimpla Kert ➤ p. 96, or try one of the lively cafés in nearby Gozsdu Court ➤ p. 54 on Kiraly utca, before returning to ① Deák Ferenc tér.

⑮ Liszt Ferenc tér

⑯ Szimpla Kert

① Deák Ferenc tér

❷ A LOOP AROUND CASTLE HILL

➤ Take the funicular up to Buda Castle
➤ Panoramic views from Matthias Church
➤ Travel through time on the cobblestones

📍	Clark Ádám tér	🏁	Clark Ádám tér
			1 day,
🔁	4.5km	🚶	1½ hrs total walking time

ℹ️ ❷ **Funicular** may be closed on Mon for maintenance, otherwise daily 8am–10pm. A ticket costs 1,200 Ft.
⓬ **Matthias Church** is often closed on Saturday afternoons for weddings. No visitors allowed on Sunday mornings during church services

ALL ABOARD! UP THE HILL BY TRAIN

❶ Clark Ádám tér

❷ Funicular

From ❶ Clark Ádám tér (by the Chain Bridge on the Buda side of the river), the nicest (if not the cheapest) way to get up Castle Hill *is to take the* ❷ funicular *(Siklό)*. During the two-minute trip it travels 101m on a 48 per cent gradient, up to *Szent György tér*. Alternatively – and for free – you can walk up in ten minutes on the path to the left of the *Siklό* starting point, past a giant mosaic of Hungary's coat of arms.

ART TREASURES AND A BROKEN HEART

❸ Buda Castle

At the funicular's top station, turn left to ❸ Buda Castle ➤ p. 34 with its excellent museums. The Hungarian National Gallery ➤ p. 34 offers an impressive exhibition of Hungarian art from the medieval period onwards. The Matthias Fountain, situated next to the building at the entrance to the History Museum's courtyard, depicts the legend of the peasant girl on the left of the fountain, Ilona (or Ilonka according to some sources), who encountered the king when he was out hunting incognito, and fell in love with him. After she discovered that she had fallen in love with a man who was beyond her reach, she is said to have died of a broken heart.

FROM PALACE TO PARADE SQUARE

Back at the funicular's top station, you will notice the neoclassical ❹ Sándor Palace *(Sándor palota),* built in 1806 and the official residence of the President of the Republic of Hungary. The neighbouring palace was a former Carmelite monastery and was transformed into Buda's first permanent theatre at the behest of Emperor Joseph II in 1790. The ❺ Castle Theatre *(Várszínház)* housed the National Dance Theatre for decades, but now the prime minister plans to use it for his new residence.

Now head along Szent György utca to Dísz tér (Parade Square), which once marked the boundary between the Castle District and the area where the commoners lived. During the Middle Ages, markets and executions were held on the square. Cosy ❻ Korona Kávéház *(daily | Dísz tér 16)* invites you to take a coffee or snack break here.

The funicular railway from Clark Ádám tér to Castle Hill

❹ Sándor Palace
❺ Castle Theatre
❻ Korona Kávéház

BREAK FOR LUNCH IN A SIDE STREET

Several streets lead off from Dísz tér, including Úri utca (Lord's Street). A little way along it, turn right onto Szentháromság utca (Holy Trinity Street), and you will notice Matthias Church ahead, which you will go past on your way back. In this lane you'll also find ❼ Jamie's Italian *(daily | Szentháromság utca 9–11 | tel. 1 8 00 92 12 | jamieoliver.com/italian/hungary),* Jamie Oliver's Italian franchise restaurant, where you can treat yourself to a lunch of antipasti and pizza on the terrace.

❼ Jamie's Italian

SENSORY DELIGHTS: ENJOY THE MOUNTAINS AND THE SOUND OF CARILLONS

❽ Tóth Árpád sétány

Return to Úri utca and cross the road to continue the walk along Szentháromság utca to ❽ Tóth Árpád sétány, a promenade on the defensive walls of Castle Hill with good views of the hills on the Buda side of the city. *Follow the promenade to the pretty Kapisztrán tér,* with the late-Gothic ❾ Magdalena Tower *(Magdolna torony),* which plays a carillon every quarter of an hour. Only the tower of the church (13th century) managed to avoid destruction in World War II. The neoclassical Museum of Military History *(Hadtörténeti Múzeum)* was once a barracks. *Behind the church tower, Országház utca heads right to the old* Regional Parliament Building. The Hungarian assembly was held here between 1785 and 1806. *Take a stroll along the narrow Kard utca to Fortuna utca. Go left to get to* Bécsi kapu tér (Vienna Gate Square). On the corner is the neoclassical ❿ Protestant church.

❾ Magdalena Tower

❿ Protestant church

IN THE FORMER JEWISH GHETTO

The northeastern part of the Castle District was the Jewish ghetto during the Middle Ages. *Its centre, Táncsics Mihály utca (junction of Bécsi kapu tér),* was commonly known as "Jewish Lane". Remnants of Jewish life in the Middle Ages are exhibited in the ⓫ Medieval Jewish House of Prayer (no. 26), which is open during the summer months. The most beautiful Baroque building on the lane is Erdődy Palace (no. 7). The street ends at the square in front of the Hilton hotel, Hess Andras tér. It owes its name to the 15th-century German painter, Andreas Hess, who is said to have produced the first book to be printed in Hungary.

⓫ Medieval Jewish House of Prayer

A FAIRYTALE CHURCH, A DREAM VIEW AND SOME MAGNIFICENT STEPS

⓬ Matthias Church

From here it is just a few steps to the ornate ⓬ Matthias Church ➤ p. 36 on Szentháromság tér (Trinity Square). The 14m-high Holy Trinity Column on the square was erected in 1715 to commemorate the ravages of the plague in 1706. Behind the church is the extremely photogenic ⓭ Fisherman's Bastion ➤ p. 36. It offers a

⓭ Fisherman's Bastion

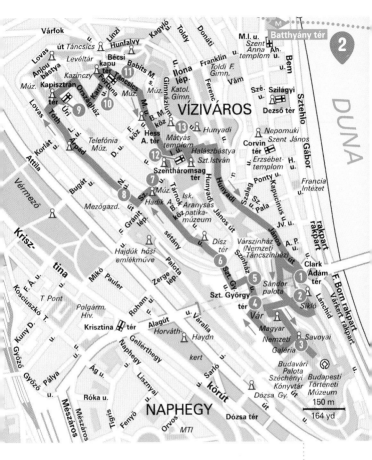

splendid view over the Danube to the Parliament Building. The large equestrian statue of King Stephen I is another work by sculptor Alajos Stróbl, who also designed the Matthias Fountain. This part of Castle Hill – with the rebuilt Matthias Church, the Fisherman's Bastion and the equestrian statue – was designed towards the end of the 19th century by Frigyes Schulek as a whole complex.

The way back leads from the Fisherman's Bastion, *down the* Royal stairs *(Király lépcső) to Hunyadi János út,* which ends at your starting point at ➊ Clark Ádám tér.

➊ Clark Ádám tér

❸ ELIZABETH TOWN: A TOUR OF THE OLD JEWISH QUARTER

➤ Discover the history of Budapest's Jews
➤ Stroll between synagogues and trendy shops
➤ Enjoy Jewish culture with *flódni* and klezmer

📍 Deák Ferenc tér

🏁 Deák Ferenc tér
½ day,

🔄 4km

🚶 1½ hrs total walking time

ℹ️ Synagogues are closed on the Sabbath (Saturday) and close earlier on Friday afternoons

❶ Deák Ferenc tér

❷ Dohány Street Synagogue

A VISIT TO THE GREAT SYNAGOGUE

The walk around the Jewish Quarter starts at the central traffic junction ❶ Deák Ferenc tér. *From there, take Károly krt* to the religious centre of the Jewish community, the splendid ❷ Dohány utca Synagogue ➤ p. 53, which was ceremonially inaugurated in 1859. Before World War II, Budapest was home to around 200,000 Jews. At the end of 1944, Elizabeth Town (Erzsébetváros) – sealed off by the Nazis and the Hungarian Arrow Cross Party from the surrounding area by a wall – became a ghetto, and for many of the thousands of Jews confined within it, also a grave. The Holocaust Memorial Centre ➤ p. 56 and the glimmering, silver Holocaust memorial by artist Imre Varga in the courtyard of the synagogue are poignant reminders of this crime.

Today there are around 80,000 Jews in Budapest, living throughout the city. But Jewish life has left many traces in Eliz-abethtown, a district in which in which Jewish religion and tra-dition have become a vital force again. You can learn more about it in the Jewish Museum housed in one of the synagogue's wings.

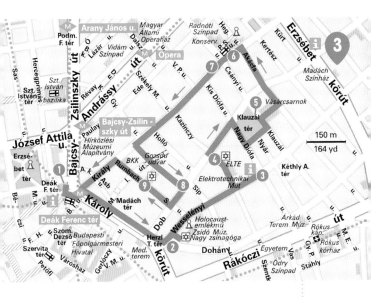

DISCOVER THE FINEST DELICACIES

From the front of the synagogue on Theodor-Herzl Square, follow Wesselényi utca. If you keep going down this street, you will pass various Jewish shops and cafés. It is worth taking a break at ③ Arán Bakery *(daily | Wesselényi utca 23),* where you can find delicious Jewish pastries such as the traditional *flódni* (layers of walnuts, apple, poppy seed and plum jam).

Finally you'll reach the Kazinczy utca. Traffic calming measures have been introduced here since it was declared a "cultural zone". To the right is the ruin pub Szimpla Kert ➤ p. 96, but *you'll go to the left where you will find* the excellently renovated ④ Orthodox Synagogue ➤ p. 54, which lies within a building complex stretching right up to Dob utca. This area is full of restaurants, cafés and pubs.

The walk now takes you right along Dob utca to Klauzál tér, where you can have a snack (such as *lángos*) in the small ⑤ indoor market hall. You can also buy some fruit, tasty cheese and bread here. *At the other end of the street, turn left along Akácfa utca to* ⑥ Terezvaros

③ Arán Bakery

④ Orthodox Synagogue

⑤ Indoor market hall
⑥ Terezvaros Parish Church

Parish Church on Király utca. The tower was built by architect Miklós Ybl (who also designed the Opera House) in 1871.

CHIC SHOPS MEET TRENDY PUBS

7 Király utca

If you now take a left along **7** Király utca *you will find yourself in the middle of a fascinating regeneration process.* A citi-zens' initiative managed to save many of the houses here from demolition, but lack of finances means that others have been left dilapidated, and some historic buildings have been replaced with faceless new structures. *Head towards Deák Ferenc tér,* in the lower part of the street, where you will find the tone is set by design shops such as Goa *(no. 21)* or the flower and decor shop Arioso *(no. 9 | arioso.hu).* Arioso also has a café with a garden that serves the most delicious macarons. After many years of decay, the wonderful complex in no. 13, Gozsdu Court ➤ p. 54, has been restored to its former glory. After luxury

INSIDER TIP
Dive into a secret garden

Where time flies: discover street art in the old Jewish Quarter

apartment lets failed to bring expected profits, numerous cafés and bars have relocated here and it's a popular destination in the evening.

FROM COFFEE TO KLEZMER

On other side of Gozsdu Court, take a right along Dob utca. On the other side of the street is ❽ Spinoza ➤ p.74, a popular address for coffee or snacks. This café-restaurant is also known for its Klezmer evenings every Friday. *Take a right at the next crossroads along Rumbach Sebestyén utca.* The beautiful ❾ Rumbach Synagogue ➤ p.53 was designed by Viennese architect Otto Wagner in 1872, in Romanesque-Moorish style.

At the end of the street, turn left into Király utca again. When the street ends, you'll see the starting point of ❶ Deák Ferenc tér to your right.

❽ Spinoza

❾ Rumbach Synagogue

❶ Deák Ferenc tér

GOOD TO KNOW

CITY BREAK BASICS

ARRIVAL

CAR

From the north and west, you can reach Budapest via motorway M1. Hungarian motorways are toll roads. Vignettes *(autópálya matrica)* – tolls based on the period of time you wish to use the road rather than distance travelled – are available at the border, at service stations and online *(maut-tarife.hu)*. They cost 3,280 Ft. for ten days and 5,210 Ft. for 31 days.

The maximum speed in Hungary in towns and cities is 50kmh, outside towns and cities it is 90kmh, and on motorways 130kmh. Outside towns you must have dipped headlights on during the day too. There is a zero-tolerance policy when it comes to drinking (the blood alcohol limit is zero) and a seatbelt must be worn on every seat. Talking on mobile phones is only permitted with a hands-free set. You must carry high-visibility jackets (one for every seat in the vehicle). In the event of a crash where people are injured, the police must be notified. Carry your insurance card.

It is no fun to be travelling in the city with a car, not least because of the lack of parking spaces. It's a better idea to leave your vehicle in the hotel garage or in a guarded car park.

BUS

There are coach connections with many cities in western Europe *(eurolines.com)*. The international bus station is *Népliget (Üllői utca 131 | metro 3: Népliget | District IX | ☷ J13)*.

PLANE

National airlines such as British Airways and Malév offer several Budapest flights a day. Among the cheaper airlines, there are flights from

Take the tram across Liberty Bridge between Buda and Pest

London and Manchester with *Easyjet* (*easyjet.com*) and *Jet2* (*jet2. com*), as well as from other western European cities. American Airlines operate direct flights from New York. *Liszt Ferenc International Airport*, with terminals 2A and 2B, is on the southeast fringes of the city.

An inexpensive way to get into the city from the airport is to take express bus 200E to the last stop on underground line 3, Kőbánya-Kispest and head into the city from there (journey time around an hour). It's a good idea to buy a multi-day travel ticket at the airport (ticket machine or the ticket desk of Budapest public transport operators BKK).

Alternatively, the 100E bus goes directly to the city centre (Kálvin tér, Astoria, Deák Ferenc tér) for 1,500 Ft. per trip.

A taxi into the city (journey time approx. 25–50 mins) will cost around 7,500 Ft., depending on your destination. The official partner of Budapest Airport is the taxi company *Főtaxi* (*fotaxi.hu/en*); there is even a fare calculator on the website and you can order online or via the app. Do not use other taxi providers (especially those without official ID).

TRAIN

Train station connections have got better and faster. The train journey from London to Budapest takes around 24 hours, by Eurostar to Paris, high-speed TGV from Paris to Munich, then railjet train (approx. 7 hrs). Alternatively, there are connections via Brussels, Cologne and Vienna. All long-distance trains arrive in Budapest at the Eastern Station (Keleti pályaudvar) (□ G9). Trains from Vienna also stop at Kelenföld (□ 0). *International train information Budapest: tel. 1 349 4999*

IMMIGRATION

US and UK citizens only need a passport to enter Hungary. US and UK visitors may stay in the country for up to 90 days for tourist or business purposes without a visa. EU citizens have free-movement rights in Hungary.

CLIMATE & WHEN TO TRAVEL

Spring and autumn are the best times to visit Budapest in terms of temperature. During the summer months the city is often extremely crowded and gets very hot. Winters can be bitterly cold, but also dry and snowy, or slushy and rainy. However, if you can put up with the chilly weather, you will be rewarded with a city far less overrun with tourists in the colder months.

RESPONSIBLE TRAVEL

The way you travel can make a real difference to the environment. You can keep track of your carbon footprint *(myclimate.org)* and plan to travel in a way that causes less damage. You can also think about how you can protect nature and culture when you're abroad *(www.ecotrans.org)*. As a tourist, it's particularly important that you consider issues such as nature conservation *(wwf.org)*, use of local products, minimal use of cars and conserving water. For more information on ecological tourism, see *ecotourism.org*.

GETTING AROUND

PUBLIC TRANSPORT

The nicest underground line, opened in 1896, is *Földalatti* (Line 1). There are three further underground lines (metro) – the red line 2, the blue line 3 and the green line 4 – as well as a dense network of trams, buses and trolley-buses.

Sightseeing for just 1.50 euros (ish): 🚋 tramline 2 takes just over 20 minutes from the Pest side of the Margaret Bridge along the Pest Danube Quay to the terminus at the Palace of Arts – with the best views of the Buda side.

There are commuter lines *(HÉV)* running along the northern right bank of the Danube (towards the Danube Bend) and along the southern left bank, as well as (in the east) towards Gödöllő. You can take a cog railway *(Fogaskerekűvasút)* into the hills around Budapest: it departs from Városmajor on the Buda side; you can also take this railway to get to the Children's Railway *(Gyermekvasút)*.

Tickets must be purchased before the journey. There are ticket machines at all metro stations and tram stops 4 and 6, for example, where you can pay by card. You have to show your ticket at most metro stations before you go down to the platforms; the same is true for some bus lines, and the bus driver will only open the front door for boarding.

One-way tickets must be validated

at the ticket machine on board or on the metro, before the escalator. You must hold on to your ticket until you have left the station, because inspectors usually stand at the exits. A single ticket (350 Ft.) is valid for the whole line, but if you switch lines, you must purchase a new ticket. It is cheaper and simpler to buy a ticket for 24 or 72 hours. a weekly ticket or a 15-day ticket (1,650/4,150/4,950/6,300 Ft., valid for all means of public transport in Budapest).

EU citizens who are pensioners (aged 65 and older) can use Hungary's public transport (buses, trains) for free. If you are checked, you must show identification. School pupils and students from the EU and Switzerland are given a 50 per cent discount by the Budapest's public transport provider, BKK (get your ID cards ready!).

Timetables and further information on public transport can be found from *BKK (underpass at Deák Ferenc tér | tel. 1 3 25 52 55 | bkk.hu | District V | ▯ d9)*.

BICYCLE
You are faster and more flexible travelling by bike than you are with public transport. The city's government is doing what it can – albeit slowly – to extend the network of cycle paths. You may also spot the bright green city bikes: to use one of these so-called *BuBi (molbubi.bkk.hu)*, you need to register at one of the 100 docking stations around the city or at outlets of the Budapest transport operator, BKK. The easiest way to hire a bike is by using a smartphone or credit card.

Tip: Once you hire a *BuBi*, the first 30 minutes are free!

Cycle tours are run by *Yellow Zebra Bike Tours (Károly körút 16 | yellow zebrabikes.com | District V | f 10)*. *Bikebase (Podmaniczky utca 19 | tel. 70 6 25 85 01 | bikebase.hu | District VI | ▯ D7)* is a good and reasonably priced bike rental service, which offers bikes and equipment for men, women or children.

RIVER TRANSPORT
It's a great idea to take a boat trip on the Danube while you're in Budapest – it will give you an amazing perspective on the city. The Budapest public transport company *BKK* and the *Mahart* shipping company jointly operate boats that cruise on a circular route on the Danube, with stops on the Buda and Pest sides as well as on Margaret Island (tickets 1,500 Ft.). Sit above in the covered area (but remember there are no windows), or head below if the weather's not great and you'd like the protection of windows!

You can also book organised boat tours and city tours by boat: *Legenda (tel. 1 2 66 41 90 | legenda.hu)* is the most popular professional provider. They offer a number of routes and options – including day and evening, and with or without a candlelit dinner – and the sights can be explained in English.

TAXI
Taxi rates are set in Budapest: the basic fare is 1,000 Ft., plus 400 Ft. per kilometre and 100 Ft. per minute of waiting time. All taxis must be

officially painted in the same shade of yellow and have a licence sticker on the side. As there are still some unscrupulous people driving around, the best idea is to phone to book a taxi: *City Taxi: tel. 1 211 1111.* Or do what the young Hungarians do and just use the app *Bolt (also tel. 1 444 5154).*

EMERGENCIES

EMBASSIES AND CONSULATES
UK EMBASSY
Füge utca 5–7 | 1022 Budapest | tel. 1 266 2888 | gov.uk/government/ world/ hungary

US EMBASSY
Szabadság tér 12 | 1054 Budapest | tel. 1 475 4400 | hu.usembassy.gov

EMERGENCY NUMBERS
Ambulance: *tel. 104* (emergency ambulance free, if an immediate medical intervention is necessary)
Police: *tel. 107,* hotline: *tel. 1 4 43 55 00*
Fire: *tel. 105*
European emergency number: *tel. 112*

ESSENTIALS

ADVANCE EVENTS TICKETS
Broadway Jegyiroda (Mon–Fri 10am–6pm | Károly körút 21 | tel. 1 7 80 07 80 | broadway.hu | metro 1, 2, 3: Deák Ferenc tér | tram 47, 48, 49 | District VII | □ d9)

Other providers include *tixa.hu, eventim.hu and jegy.hu*

BUDAPEST CARD
The *Budapest Card* (available at venues including airports and at the Budapest Tourist Office) gives you unlimited use of public transport and offers a wealth of further advantages and reductions. For example, you can use the small electric shuttle buses *(Official Budapest Castle Bus)* that travel the short, steep route between Clark Ádám tér and the Castle District free of charge. It costs 5,500 Ft. (29 hrs), 8,500 Ft. (48 hrs) or 10,900 Ft. (72 hrs). *More info and online order: budapestinfo.hu*

CITY TOURS
You can book city tours *(városnézés)* for day or night, tours of the Hungarian Parliament Building and trips to Buda Castle in English in hotels, travel agencies and tourist offices, or online. There are tours on Segways, electric scooters and even buses that can transform into boats and float on the Danube *(riverride.hu).*

City tours, some in open buses, are run by international providers such as *Hop-on-Hop-off (hoponhop off-budapest.com)* and *Big Bus Tours (bigbustours.com/en/Budapest).* You'll bump into their staff at all the major sights, but for the people of Budapest, this type of city tour usually means stress and extra traffic. If possible, it's best to opt for more sustainable forms of tourism, such as free walking

INSIDER TIP
Eco-friendly tours

tours *(triptobudapest.hu)*. The idea is that there is no set price but that you tip the (Hungarian, usually young) guides at the end of the tour depending on how satisfied you were.

Other recommended local providers offering themed city tours (in English) include *Hosszú Lépés (hosszulepes. org/en)* and *Imagine Budapest (imaginebudapest.hu)*. The private tours offered by *Cold War Private Tours Budapest (coldwarbudapest. com)* take the tour experience to the next level: the organisers have spent years researching and uncovering the dark history of US spies in Cold War Hungary.

CUSTOMS
Goods for personal consumption can be imported and exported for free within the EU. Non-commercial quantities of items are not subject to custom duties in Hungary but may be subject to the custom duties and import regulations of a destination country outside the EU. For UK rules, check *www.gov.uk*. For US rules, see *www.cbp.gov*.

INFORMATION
BUDAPEST FESTIVAL AND TOURIST CENTRE (BFTK)
Városháza park | metro 1, 2, 3: Deák Ferenc tér | District V | ⬚ d9
Liget visitor centre on Dózsa György út | metro 1 Hősök tere (Heroes' Square) | District XIV | ⬚ G6
Airport Liszt Ferenc: Terminal 2A and 2B | bus 200E, 100E | ⬚ 0
Website: budapestinfo.hu

HOW MUCH DOES IT COAST?

Cappuccino	*£1.22/$1.72 per cup*
Lunch menu	*approx. £ 2.60–£6.97/$3.68–$9.80 for a lunch menu in a restaurant*
Beer	*£1.22/$1.72 per glass (0.5 litres)*
Taxi	*£0.78/$1.10 per kilometre*
Metro	*£12.35/$15.50 for a 72-hour ticket incl. the regional network*
Thermal baths	*£11/$16 for a day ticket, incl. changing cubicle*

INTERNET ACCESS & WIFI
The density of WiFi hotspots is generally high. There is free WiFi in almost all cafés (and chain coffeehouses), restaurants and pubs in the inner city as well as in shopping centres (such as Westend in Pest and Mammut in Buda). The airport also has free WiFi.

LUGGAGE STORAGE
Store suitcases, rucksacks and other items safely and centrally at *Luggage Storage Budapest Hi5 (daily 9am–7pm | Fehér Hajó utca 8–10 | luggage storagebudapest.com)*. Ring the bell outside and the actual storage is located in the inner courtyard.

MEDIA

International daily newspapers are available especially at *Inmedio* news-agents (branches have a red sign and include *Városház utca 3–5, near Ferenciek tere*), from kiosks in the touristy areas in the city centre (Vörösmarty tér, Váci utca) and in large hotels. The *Budapest Times (budapest-times.hu)* is Hungary's leading English-language source for daily news, restaurants, hotels, movies, culture and tourism. TV satellite channels are accessible everywhere. Read high-quality journalism about Hungary in English on the website of the largest Hungarian online newspaper *Telex (telex.hu/english)*. Plenty of tips and many of the city's restaurants and bars are listed on *welovebudapest.com/en*.

MONEY & CREDIT CARDS

The currency in Hungary is the forint (Ft., HUF). Changing money is possible in banks, travel agencies, bureaux de change and through money-changing machines (in banks). Be careful with the bureaux de change at the airport and in the city centre as the exchange rate is often very unfavourable. Banks are usually open Mon–Thu 8am–6pm and Fri 8am–3pm. You will also be able to get money with the usual credit/debit cards at banks and ATMs. And you can pay with your credit card almost everywhere (supermarkets, restaurants, pubs, taxis), and use contactless with the Paypass system. Currency converters can be found online, for example at *oanda. com*.

NATIONAL HOLIDAYS

1 Jan	New Year's Day
15 March	Day of the Hungarian Revolution of 1848
March/April (dates vary)	Good Friday
March/April (dates vary)	Easter Monday
1 May	Labour Day
May (dates vary)	Whit Monday
20 Aug	St Stephen's Day23 Oct Republic Day, commemorating the 1956 uprising
1 Nov	All Saints' Day
25/26 Dec	Christmas

OPENING HOURS

Specialist shops are usually open Mon–Fri from 10am to 6pm and on Saturdays between 10am and 1pm. Bigger shops, shopping centres and supermarkets often have longer opening times and sometimes open on Sundays. Museums are usually open Tue–Sun from 10am to 6pm, but often close earlier in winter at 4pm.

PHONES & MOBILES

Phone numbers in Budapest have seven digits, and the city dialling code is 1. For a local call from a landline you can omit the 1. From a landline in Hungary but outside Budapest, as well as from Hungarian mobile phones, you have to dial 06 as well as the area code, so for Budapest you dial 061, followed by the phone number.

The country dialling code for Hungary is 0036; if you want to call a Budapest number from a landline outside of Hungary, you have to dial 00361, then the phone number. Hungarian mobile phone numbers also have seven digits and usually start with 20, 30 or 70. To call one from a Hungarian landline or mobile, you always have to prefix it by 06 (eg 0620, then the seven-digit number). To call the UK, dial 0044, to call the USA, dial 001, then the local area code minus the 0 and then the phone number.

POST

Post offices are generally open Mon–Fri 8am 6pm and Sat 8am–noon. The postage for standard letters and post-cards to European countries is 635 Ft. The post office in the Mammut shopping centre is open Mon–Fri until 8pm and Sat/Sun until 2pm.

TIPS & SERVICE CHARGES

A tip of 10 per cent is customary in restaurants and pubs, but it's not expected when you order at the bar. Restaurants (but not snack bars) are allowed to levy a service charge of up to 15 per cent, which will be shown on the bill. That's not the norm, but it never hurts to be vigilant if you don't want to pay end up tipping twice.

WEATHER IN BUDAPEST

■■■ High season
■■■ Low season

	JAN	FEB	MARCH	APRIL	MAY	JUNE	JULY	AUG	SEPT	OCT	NOV	DEC
Daytime temperature	2°	4°	11°	17°	22°	26°	28°	27°	23°	16°	8°	3°
Night-time temperature	-3°	-2°	2°	6°	11°	14°	16°	15°	12°	7°	3°	-1°
Sunshine hours/day	2	3	4	6	8	8	9	9	7	5	2	1
Rainy days/month	8	7	7	7	9	8	7	6	6	8	9	9

☀ Sunshine hours/day   🌧 Rainy days/month

WORDS & PHRASES IN HUNGARIAN

SMALL TALK

yes/no/maybe	**igen/nem/talán**
please	**kérem**
thank you	**köszönöm**
good morning/day/evening/night!	**Jó reggelt!/napot!/estét!/éjszakát!**
hello/goodbye!	**Halló!/Viszontlátásra!**
hi/hi there!	**Szia; Sziasztok!**
I am called ...	**...-nak hívnak.**
What's your name? (informal, formal)?	**Hogy hívnak?/Hogy hívják Önt?**
Excuse me! (informal, formal)	**Bocsáss meg!/Bocsásson meg, kérem!**
Sorry	**sajnálom**
I (don't) like that	**Ez (nem) tetszik.**

SYMBOLS

EATING & DRINKING

The menu, please.	**Az étlapot kérem.**
Could I please have some ... ?	**Hozna nekem kérem ...?**
salt/pepper/sugar	**só/bors/cukor**
vinegar/oil	**ecet/olaj**
milk/cream/lemon	**tej/tejszín/citrom**
with ice/without ice/carbonated	**jéggel/jég nélkül/szénsavas**
vegetarian/allergy	**vegetáriánus/allergia**
I would like to pay, please.	**Fizetni szeretnék, kérem.**
bill/receipt	**számla/nyugta**
cash/credit card	**készpénz/hitelkártya**

MISCELLANEOUS

Where is .../Where are ...?	**Hol van ...?/** **Hol vannak ...?**
May I take a photo here?	**Szabad itt fényképezni?**
What time is it?	**Hány óra (van)?**
today/tomorrow/yesterday	**ma/holnap/tegnap**
How much is ...?	**Mennyibe kerül ...?**
open/closed	**nyitva/zárva**
cheap/expensive	**olcsó/drága**
timetable/ticket	**menetrend/menetjegy**
Internet access	**internethozzáférés**
pharmacy/drugstore	**gyógyszertár/drogéria**
broken/out of order	**rossz/nem működik**
breakdown/garage	**defekt/műhely**
ban/banned	**tilalom/tilos**
0/1/2/3/4/5/6/7/8/9/10/ 100/1000	**nulla/egy/kettő; két/három/négy/** **öt/hat/hét/nyolc/kilenc/tíz/száz/** **ezer**

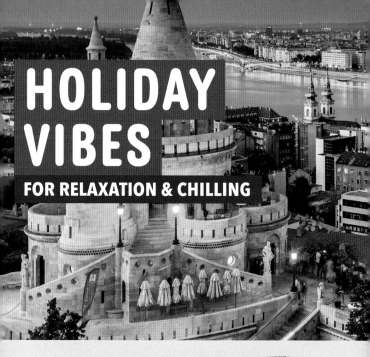

HOLIDAY VIBES

FOR RELAXATION & CHILLING

FOR BOOKWORMS & FILM BUFFS

📖 THE MONSTER

You don't need to have read *The Only Man on the Continent* to be hooked by this sequel novel from Terézia Moras. The novel's hero, Darius, travels to Budapest and other places in search of the truth about his late wife. (2013)

🎥 MOSZKVA TÉR

This debut film from Ferenc Töröks is a cult favourite in Hungary. Set in the summer of 1989, it centres around Buda's Moszkva tér (Moscow Square) – the meeting place for the film's young protagonists. The square was renamed Széll Kálmán tér in 2011, but for the people of Budapest it seems likely to remain Moszkva tér. (2001)

📖 BUDAPEST NOIR

Hungarian crime writer Vilmos Kondor transports you to another world with this exciting noir-style thriller. The protagonist, police reporter Zsigmond Gordon, finds himself with a shocking case to solve in 1936 Budapest. (2010)

🎥 FOR SOME INEXPLICABLE REASON

This feature film by director Gábor Reisz is about a film student named Áron. It's funny, honest and very Hungarian in style. A viewing is highly recommended to get you in the mood for your trip to Budapest. (2014)

PLAYLIST ON SHUFFLE

0:58

⏸ **PANNONIA ALLSTARS SKA ORCHESTRA** – BUDAPEST
Set to great ska music, the lyrics of this song (2009) play on the wonderful contradictions of the capital city to great effect.

▶ **KARSAY DOROTTYA** – NEM TETSZIK A RENDSZER
This song's title translates to "I don't like the system". Dating back to 2011, it was written by a group of activists and is directed at the Fidesz party.

*Your holiday soundtrack can be found on **Spotify** under **MARCO POLO Hungary***

▶ **ILLÉS** – KERESEM A SZÓT
Popular beat band form the 1960s and 1970s. Frontman Lajos Illés sings about love – of course.

▶ **SZABÓ BALÁZS BANDÁJA** – KÖZELEBB
Unpretentious folk and pop with beautiful lyrics (2012).

▶ **KARÁDY KATALIN** – JÓ ÉJT BUDAPEST
"Good night, Budapest": a magical piece from the 1940s.

Or scan this code with the Spotify app

ONLINE

BKK FUTÁR
This app from Budapest's public transport authority uses GPS to show you all the available public transport options in the immediate vicinity.

BOLT
Easy-to-use app that allows you to hail a carbon-neutral taxi right then and there – all without having to explain where you are.

OFFBEATBUDAPEST.COM
Hungarian Tobias Tas writes about the lesser-known gastronomic and cultural sides of Budapest (in English) and keeps his Facebook and Instagram pages up to date with the latest info.

BUDAPEST DESIGN MAP
English-language app developed for Budapest Design Week 2016, with fab tips on design hotspots. A must-have!

WELOVEBUDAPEST.COM
Budapest by season, the restaurant scene, photos, events and much more: this English-language website is packed with useful city-related gems.

TRAVEL PURSUIT
THE MARCO POLO HOLIDAY QUIZ

Do you know what makes Budapest tick? Test your knowledge of the idiosyncrasies and eccentricities of the city and its people. You'll find the answers at the foot of the page, with more detailed explanations on pages 20 to 25.

❶ The Hungarian word for "quick-witted" is *talpraesett* and literally translates as "fallen on your …"?
a) Hands
b) Feet
c) Back

❷ What smells like rotten eggs in Budapest?
a) The cave system in Castle Hill
b) The Danube on summer days
c) The sulphurous water in the thermal baths

❸ Which of these was invented by a Hungarian?
a) The typewriter
b) The computer
c) The ballpoint pen

❹ Who traditionally whiled away the hours in the coffee houses of Budapest?
a) Writers, journalists and artists
b) River boatmen
c) Tea merchants

❺ Which of the following is an actual Hungarian word?
a) Nejnezdevětadevadesáteroznás-obovávatelnějšími
b) Megszentségteleníthetetlensé-geskedéseitekért
c) Muvaffakiyetsizleştiricileştiriverem-eyebileceklerimizdenmişsinizcesinesi niz

The Café Gerbeaud is legendary, but who used to frequent Budapest's coffee houses?

❻ What have some critics dubbed Prime Minister Orbán's regime?
a) Orbánistan
b) Fidesz country
c) Goulash dictatorship

❼ What is Hungary's answer to saffron?
a) A curry blend
b) Vanilla pods
c) Powdered paprika

❽ What often crops up in the hidden courtyards and empty buildings of Budapest?
a) Tent rentals
b) Ruin pubs
c) Mobile libraries

❾ What is unique about Hungarian Art Nouveau?
a) Its conspicuous lack of ornamentation
b) Its ornamental decadence
c) It has its own architectural language

❿ Are there thermal water caves in Budapest?
a) Yes, a lot
b) Yes, but not many
c) No, just thermal baths

⓫ Why is the Danube the secret star of the show on the national holiday for St Stephen's Day?
a) That's when the annual dragon boat festival takes place
b) It reflects the enormous fireworks display
c) That's when the Danube Carnival is celebrated

INDEX

WE WANT TO HEAR FROM YOU!

Did you have a great holiday? Is there something on your mind? Whatever it is, let us know! Whether you want to praise the guide, alert us to errors or give us a personal tip – MARCO POLO would be pleased to hear from you. Please contact us by email:

sales@heartwoodpublishing.co.uk

We do everything we can to provide the very latest information for your trip. Nevertheless, despite all of our authors' thorough research, errors can creep in. MARCO POLO does not accept any liability for this.

PICTURE CREDITS
Cover photo: Calvinist Church, Szilagyi Dezso ter 3, Budapest (huber-images: L. Debelkova)

Photos: huber-images: M. Borchi (2/3, 17, 48), L. Debelkova (12/13, 138/139), M. Ripani (117), R. Schmid (6/7, 40, 43, 68, 78/79), R. Taylor (110/111), TC (56, 83, 84, 95, 97), L. Vaccarella (9, 26/27, 37, 112/113); Laif: Barth (89), E. Häberle (22), Hahn (121), G. Lengler (35, 126/127), J. Modrow (73), P. Rigaud (67), D. Schwelle (86, 90/91), B. Steinhilber (106/107), Stukhard (100), A. Volgyi (98, 108/109); Laif/SZ Photo: J. Giribas (140/141); Look: E. Fleisher (46, 62/63), I. Pompe (24); Look/age fotostock (11); mauritius images/Alamy: T. G. Bencomo (front outside flap, front inside flap/1), M. G. Casella (61), EFesenko (52), R. Johnson (31), W. Lemlerkchai (21), Piya Travel (71), M. Slusarczyk (59), Soma (77); mauritius images/imagebroker/Funkystock: P. Williams (14/15); mauritius images/Photononstop (45); mauritius images/robertharding (104/105); mauritius images/Travel Collection (32); picture-alliance: K. Rose (10); picture-alliance/EPA-EFE: Z. Szigetvary (103); picture-alliance/picturedesk.com: R. Newald (74); picture-alliance/Shotshop: Givaga (4), JB (8); Shutterstock: RossHelen (128/129); L. Weil (143)

5th Edition fully revised and updated 2024
Worldwide Distribution: Heartwood Publishing Ltd, Bath, United Kingdom
www.heartwoodpublishing.co.uk

Authors: Rita Stiens, Lisa Weil
Editor: Corinna Walkenhorst
Picture editor: Anja Schlattere
Cartography: © MAIRDUMONT, Ostfildern (pp. 114–115, 118–119, 123, 125, inside cover, outside cover, pull-out main map);
© MAIRDUMONT, Ostfildern; Hallwag Kümmerly+Frey AG, CH-Schönbühl/Bern (pull-out secondary maps)
© MAIRDUMONT, Ostfildern, using data from OpenStreetMap, licence CC-BY-SA 2.0 (pp. 28–29, 33, 38, 47, 51, 55, 58, 64–65, 80–81, 92–93)
Cover design and pull-out map cover design: bilekjaeger_Kreativagentur with Zukunftswerkstatt, Stuttgart
Page design: Langenstein Communication GmbH, Ludwigsburg

Heartwood Publishing credits:
Translated from the German by Madeleine Taylor-Laidler and Susan Jones
Editors: Rosamund Sales, Kate Michell, Felicity Laughton, Sophie Blacksell Jones
Prepress: Summerlane Books, Bath
Printed in India

MARCO POLO AUTHOR
LISA WEIL

Born in Stuttgart to Hungarian parents, Lisa Erzsa Weil discovered during her studies at Budapest's ELTE University that it *is* possible to have two homelands after all. For a start, Hungary has its own version of German *spaetzle* noodles, known as *galuska*. So she felt right at home! Today, Lisa lives and works in Budapest as a journalist, translator, copywriter and concept developer.

DOS & DON'TS

HOW TO AVOID SLIP-UPS & BLUNDERS

DON'T EXCHANGE MONEY ON THE STREET

It's illegal to change money on the street, and the danger of being scammed is high or you may be robbed when you whip out your wallet. Don't be tempted to buy items such as iPhones and perfume on the street, either: you could easily become a victim of fraud.

DON'T LEAVE YOUR CAR UNATTENDED

Park your car for the duration of your stay in a safe car park and never leave valuable objects or documents in it. Book a space in a car park with surveillance at *ezparkbudapest.com*.

DON'T TAKE DRUGS

No doubt about it: keep your hands off the marijuana, ecstasy and other illegal drugs. Firstly, party drugs are often laced with other substances, which makes their effect extremely unpredictable. Secondly, Hungary has strict laws on drugs: if you are caught in possession, you can face up to two years in prison.

DON'T GET POLITICAL

Although Budapest voted in a green-left-liberal mayor in 2019, you won't struggle to find those eager to express very conservative or even far-right opinions. To avoid an unpleasant argument, don't discuss controversial issues with taxi drivers and others.

DO CHECK FOR HIDDEN COSTS

In the past, Budapest restaurants and bars in tourist areas were unfortunately notorious for charging extortionate prices. Always check the bill before paying, and when bread is brought to the table ask whether it's free, for example.